Life After Life

A Grieving Daughter's Healing Chats with her father

Life After Life

A Grieving Daughter's
Healing Chats with her
Father

Also by the author

Estate Sales Made Easy – A Practical Guide from Start to Finish

The Secret Vision – The Richness of Thought (fall 2019)

My Past Life with Henry Ford (December 2019)

Body Etiquette – Move with Ease ebook at: www.victoriagray.net

Victoria Gray Unfolded: The Speaking Linens

The Ankle Express - Life and Times of Wm. Victor Gray

Life After Life

A Grieving Daughter's Healing Chats...with her Father

VICTORIA GRAY

GRAY PUBLISHING, USA

Copyright © 2019 by Victoria Gray

Published and distributed in the United States by: Gray Publishing

Cover design: Victoria Gray
Interior design: Victoria Gray: All rights reserved.
Number sequence by: *Joanne Walmsley,* Sacred Scribes, Intuitive Writer & Lightworker, Information, Inspiration, Enlightenment, Empowerment
Victoria Australia

No part of this book may be reproduced by any mechanical, photographic, or electronic process, or in the form of a phonographic recording; nor may it be stored in a retrieval system, transmitted, or otherwise be copied for public or private use—other than for "fair use" as brief quotations embodied in articles and reviews—without prior written permission of the publisher.

The author of this book does not dispense medical advice or prescribe the use of any technique as a form of treatment for physical, emotional, or medical problems without the advice of a physician, either directly or indirectly. The intent of the author is only to offer information of a general nature to help you in your quest for emotional, physical, and spiritual wellbeing. In the event you use any of the information in this book for yourself, the author and the publisher assume no responsibility for your actions.

Library of Congress Cataloging-in-Publication Data TK

Tradepaper ISBN: 978-1-7978-7095-3

10 9 8 7 6 5 4 3 2 1

1st edition, 2019

Printed in the United States of America

To Rachel, Caleb, Blake & Ashley, Edmond

And new little girl on the way!

May you always pay attention to what is!

In memory of my father, Wm. Victor Gray,

Who graciously answers my questions at a moment's notice!

Of course, there are no time constraints from beyond.

Love you all forever and always!!!!

CONTENTS

INTRODUCTION i

Chapter One	A Chat with Dad	1
Chapter Two	Freedoms importance to me	17
Chapter Three	Angels among us	25
Chapter Four	A Silent Knowing	37
Chapter Five	Children Born on Earth	41
Chapter Six	A Simple Cup of Tea	47
Chapter Seven	Spiritual Foot Print & Galaxies	51
Chapter Eight	Something More	63
Chapter Nine	Family & Obstacles	67
Chapter Ten	Dreams...Spirituality Optimus and Spisterterious	77
Chapter Eleven	Karma and the Bible	87
Chapter Twelve	De-ja-vu...Stars...Going Forward	99
Chapter Thirteen	Family...Past Lives & Patrick Henry	109
Chapter Fourteen	Skeptism	123
Chapter Fifteen	Gnats...Butterflies...Seeing Energies	127
Chapter Sixteen	Listen is the Key	135
Introduction Symbols deciphered		145
List of those that Came Forward		158
About the Author		159

Introduction....

Friday evening, August 3rd, 2012, Dad wanted to revisit the local pizza restaurant he and mom often visited over the past twenty or so years, but now he'd almost quit driving, thus his call, "Honey, would you mind taking us to Happy Joe's for dinner? We're ready to go!"

"Well, sure. I just finished working."

"Will Blake come with you?"

"Yes, I just asked him."

"Great, let's get out of here!"

I picked them up around seven. Just like dad, he smiled from ear to ear, excited to leave the house. Mom had dementia and knew not where we were going; however, she always liked to go. So off we went to the pizza parlor. When we walked in, I noticed dad was slightly shaking, which was unlike him. The manager, Norm greeted and seated us with his usual smile, shook dad's hand and said, "This man is our best customer! We all love him. Some in the back saw you come in Vic and said hello. We all miss you."

Dad shook his hand, cried, which made me and Norm tear up.

Norm went back to get us a free beer, but when he came back with them, dad had just told me he needed to get out of there. He was feeling sick. Immediately, I told Blake to stay there, and I'd take dad home. We'd already paid for our food, so Blake and mom stayed to eat. I'd be back soon.

Now at the family home, dad sat in his massage chair, rocking forward and backward. I asked if he thought he might be having a heart attack. He said, "*No honey; I think I might have indigestion.*" He told me to pick up mom and Blake; *"I'll be ok"*.

"Really?"

"Yes, please get them."

Our family home is maybe two miles from the pizza place and within fifteen minutes or less, I returned home with them.

When I returned home, I called my cousin Dr. Clem Haggerty, one of the head doctors at the Lake of the Ozarks Hospital asking, what do I do?

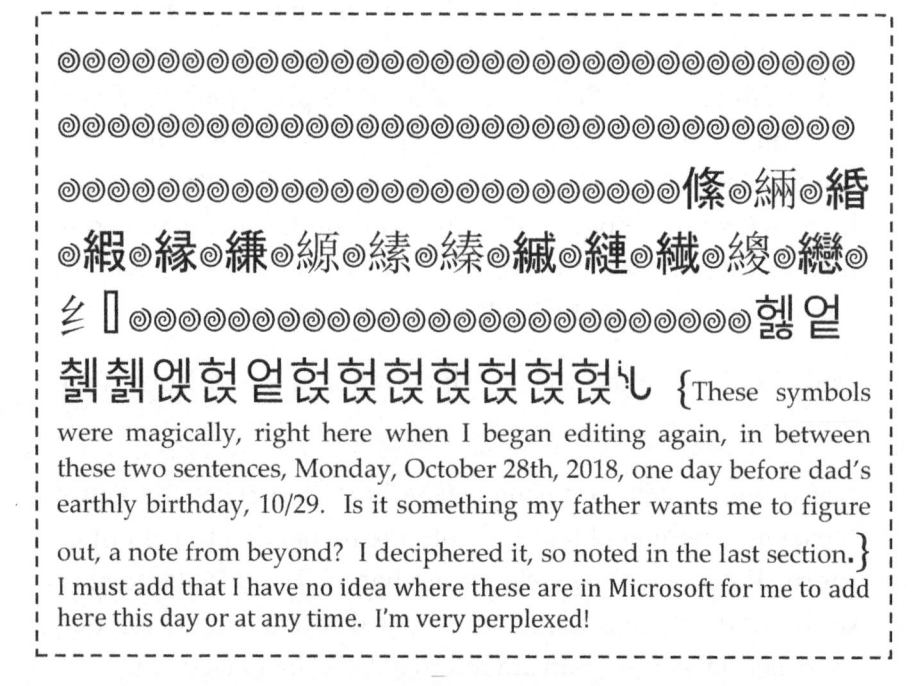

⊚⊚⊚⊚⊚⊚⊚⊚⊚⊚⊚⊚⊚⊚⊚⊚⊚⊚⊚⊚⊚⊚⊚⊚⊚
⊚⊚⊚⊚⊚⊚⊚⊚⊚⊚⊚⊚⊚⊚⊚⊚⊚⊚⊚⊚⊚⊚⊚⊚⊚
⊚⊚⊚⊚⊚⊚⊚⊚⊚⊚⊚⊚⊚⊚⊚⊚⊚條⊚緉⊚縉⊚緞⊚緣⊚縑⊚線⊚繡⊚縥⊚緘⊚縫⊚織⊚縫⊚戀⊚
糸 ▯⊚⊚⊚⊚⊚⊚⊚⊚⊚⊚⊚⊚⊚⊚⊚⊚⊚⊚⊚헳 얼
췍췍엣헝얼헝헝헝헝헝헝헝ㄴ {These symbols were magically, right here when I began editing again, in between these two sentences, Monday, October 28th, 2018, one day before dad's earthly birthday, 10/29. Is it something my father wants me to figure out, a note from beyond? I deciphered it, so noted in the last section.}
I must add that I have no idea where these are in Microsoft for me to add here this day or at any time. I'm very perplexed!

He asked me, "Did Uncle Victor take Mylanta?"

"No Tums."

"Okay, then give him a ¼ glass of milk, wait thirty minutes. Do this two times. If no difference, take him to the hospital."

"Goodness!"

I called my eldest brother asking him to drive over to the house to stay with mom and to call our siblings; thus he arrived within twenty minutes. Subsequently, I called all my kids too.

I did just what he the doctor said, but no difference. A quick ride to the hospital and two hours later the doctors determined he had a major heart attack.

I'm so thankful I was there with dad when the heart attack began and ended. My sister Penny and I stayed the night, she till 4 a.m. and I till 7 a.m. then I had to go to work by 9 a.m.

Dad, in true dad fashion, while a robust young nurse readied his bed and bent over, he slapped her on her butt! I heard a loud pop, turned around and silly dad said, "Honey, it was just there", smiling all the while. That nurse, another nurse and I filled the room with uncontrollable laughter! The nurse that he popped said, "He's going to be fun to work with!"

I said, "Now this is my dad!"

At work the following day, a customer named Milton, a generally gruff man asked how I was. As I reiterated the story of my father's heart attack, the night before, tears I tried to hold back, streamed down my face. This man's voice softened and became sympathetic, stating, "Always remember the good times. You've been blessed to have him sixty years."

I had extreme difficulty holding back heaving shoulder rocking tears, and yet I managed to say, 'Indeed I have! Thank you, I will remember the good times."

Dad had many family and friends, which showed up in scores each day at the hospital. The staff told me that no one ever had so many in the ICU.

Indeed, dad was just that special.

August 5th, 2012, at the hospital, the doctors told us this might be his last day. I prayed off and on all day, *please Universe, Lord, Angels; take dad another day and not on my brother Dwayne's birthday*! Thankfully, the mighty powers that be, answered my prayers.

Soon, the doctors informed us that dad had numerous mini-strokes that came and went, which meant he wouldn't be with us much longer. Hence dad told the doctors that he didn't want life support and wanted to go home to finish his last days with his babies.

August 6th, 2012, dad still in intensive care where the nurses again stated they'd never seen so many people visit anyone, ever in intensive care, I asked, "Should all leave?"

"Oh no, this is wonderful." Of course, the family would have stayed regardless.

This same day, the doctor placed dad on a morphine drip to thwart off the pain from the mini-strokes. Everyone was extremely thankful! Because the morphine drip had such a strong dosage, dad began to hallucinate. I arrived at the hospital around 4 p.m. this day and after hugging my dad, I stepped out of his room to visit with my cousin Ladonna Weber and her daughter Brenda, who just arrived. They loved dad too and were very heartbroken.

After visiting with them a few minutes, I returned to dad's room to hear him ask me, "Well Vickie, did you fly here? You know he (Charles Lindbergh) built that plane by hand?" {I researched to see if Mr. Lindbergh actually constructed the Spirit of St Louis plane. He did not; however it was custom built by Ryan Airlines in California.}

"No, I drove here."

He continued, "Oh, honey its history! It's so special!" He hit his bed on both sides of his body with a dynamic resonating sound displaying excitement of the possibility of seeing Mr. Lindbergh.

He continued, "Can you believe it? He will call soon. I need to get out of this bed and get dressed."

I said, "No, dad, stay in bed. He'll talk to you there. Ok?"

He replied, "Ok, I guess so."

While I visited my cousins just beyond dad's room, I wasn't privy to the fact that he'd began to hallucinate, out of his head, when he spoke of Charles Lindbergh. Here's what they said he stated, "I'm to receive a call from him anytime. Let's not get puffed up – let's stay balanced. We need to be calm, and everyone needs to be kind to one another." My brother, Dwayne, stated dad called him Mr. Lindbergh. My perception of this Lindbergh call and encounter told me that dad was now very close to the other side.

Within minutes, one of the nieces leaned over dad's left side, I on the right and said, "Papa, you know when the elder from the Jehovah's Witness church was here yesterday, he said life is like a fairy tale, and you're at the end of the fairy tale. You need to go to the other side, the other side to Paradise."

I knew the Jehovah Witness church I attended from youth, up till age thirty-six, taught all about a fairytale existence after death and or living through the fictitious story of Armageddon. I also thought she and that man were crazy! She'd become a thorn in my side at the hospital and later at dad's home, a very disrespectful childlike girl in her early twenties. At one point, dad apparently, heard me tell this rebellious girl that I'd like to have some time with my father and yet she would not leave the room. I steamed inside and in my warm firm tone, asked her to allow me my time with my father. She withdrew! But dad said, "Honey, try to be balanced, they love me too." He, of course, was correct. I had work to do on me. Whether they respected me or not, I respect my father.

Then her father leaned over by my dad to say, "You know Vic you'll be in a better place soon."

Dad placed his hands over his face and cried and said, "Let's just back off now." Even on his deathbed, he'd had enough. I swung my right arm towards this jerk, hitting his sleeve to say, "Stop it now! He doesn't need to hear that." He stopped and walked out of the room.

I called my two older children, one in California and the other in Pennsylvania for dad to chat a final time with them. My babies and all of us cried and cried; pleased they had a chance to speak to dad, but ever so disheartened that this precious, loved-by-all man, would soon leave us.

After we left, this night, the doctors took him off life support; then called us stating that he might have another heart attack and die within a few hours. We all quickly drove back to the hospital, of which he made it through the night.

Tuesday, August 7th, 2012, dad, now on the eighth floor, and before returning home to live out his remaining days, was polite to everyone that came and went, shedding many tears this day. That was my father, kind, gentle and ever so pleasant to one and all!

Wednesday, August 8th, 2012, dad had another heart attack! The family constantly at his bedside every day, either before or after work and some of us just took off to be there.

In the mix, several grandchildren visited him that still attended the church of my youth, as aforementioned, believing in a paradise where all pass to, when we die. I'm okay with that, however; one of them continually reminded dad of a paradise where he'd no longer feel pain, all the while rubbing her thumb up and down his forehead for half an hour straight! This constant rubbing of my father's head bothered my daughter and me so much so that at one point I said, "Why don't we let papa rest, let's leave." I just wanted dad and his forehead to have a break! She would not go, and she did not quit rubbing a hole in his forehead!

A few minutes later I asked her if she'd mind if I spent a few minutes with my father. Amazed, that she got the massive hint, she left! Ah, I had maybe twelve minutes alone with my treasured father.

Dad said, "Honey; you're such a good woman. I love you so much. But try not to let them make you mad and remember to be balanced. They love me too."

Oh my! Dad heard everything!

I told him I'd try. He knows I'm like him; in that we don't take any baloney!

I had a very trying day, indeed!

By Friday, August 10th, all dads' babies were present, and he beamed. When I leaned in to tell him I loved him; softly he said, "You're the one to bear the hard times. It may be hot, it may be cold, but you can do it!" Dad, a very astute, kind and gentle man to the very end, knew his Bixby (a sweet nickname dubbed me by dad when I was a little girl) and what she's had to deal with over the years. Yes, I can and did handle the hot and the cold. It's incredible what ugliness comes forth from family members when a loved one is dying and dies.

Saturday, August 11th, dad, still his beautiful self, his eyes widened as I walked into the room at which time he said, "I smell a little Vickie." He smiled, looked down with a sheepish grin I often saw, so endearing, so cute! My youngest daughter Ashley, with me, later said, "Mom you're the only one he called by name!"

Sweet, my buddy, my father.

Throughout his last days now at the family home, often he said, "I want to leave this life like a man. I can take it." Four days before dad died and an hour or so before he slipped into a coma, I leaned into his right cheek and said, "Dad, I'll miss you so much and the rubbing of your whiskers on my face." He quickly rubbed his whiskered face up and down my right cheek; with a week raspy voice said, "Take that with you." That was the last thing he said to anyone. Weak sorrowful smiles, we hugged, and I fell apart!

Monday, August 20th, 2012, I received a call from my nephew that Papa just died. We gave him his morphine at 3:29 a.m., fifteen minutes later, he stopped breathing.

The love of my life just left.

My heart; broken.

I've had the gift of his existence for sixty-and-a-half years; selfishly I wanted more. Who will I chat with concerning in-depth subjects? My kids of course; nevertheless, my special father, now removed from his earthly journey, won't be available.

The night before, my son Blake and I, and my younger sister spent eight hours at his bedside till 8 p.m. Our youngest sister and a grandson then took their shift and stayed overnight.

Dad had gone into a coma the Thursday before and quit eating a few days before that. It was his last request that he die in our family home, a wish we all respected.

My two daughters, Rachel and Ashley were present. My son Caleb, in California, had spoken to papa just before the coma, to say his last goodbyes. My son Blake, in St. Louis said his goodbye's Sunday afternoon along with me.

It was a very wistful morning. Dad, the hub of our family, was gone. He represented a towering strength, like a large oak tree that sheltered us when nothing else ever could, with the power of Samson and the kindness of a lamb.

My best friend; gone.

The hospice care woman had been called and arrived soon after all of us. I live twenty minutes away. My eldest daughter Rachel, one and a half hours south of St. Louis and my youngest daughter, Ashley also about twenty minutes away. All siblings were there as well. A few other grandchildren were also present. One claimed to be a nurse; however, she never worked as one, and continuously tried to keep dad's children from helping dress him or whatever needed to be done. She, a young woman of twenty-two with a take on life like a fourteen-year old, sheltered, childlike mind thought she knew everything, and yet no wisdom to back it up.

The hospice care lady looked to me, the eldest daughter asking if this granddaughter had any experience. She did not. I wanted to dress my father for his ride to his cremation. I was thwarted away by this young know-it-all! I didn't want to cause a scene; however my youngest daughter, Ashley said, "Mom, will help Papa." The girl angered, tore off her blue gloves as if papa was filled with germs and left the room.

I walked over to my sweet father unclad of blue gloves to say in his ear "Bixby is here. I'll dress you. All is well. We love you and will miss the heck out of you my sweet!" Of course, tears flowed as I spoke to him one last time, so I thought.

I followed the hospice ladies guidance. We dressed dad in his favorite short sleeved baby blue dress shirt, black pants, black socks and one of his favorite ties, which was navy blue with small white dots. I combed his hair.

Soon after that, the hearse arrived to take away my/our precious father.

All siblings followed the two men carrying dad out on the stretcher, now entombed in a black zippered case.

Dad is gone; this is indeed final. We five hugged in a huddle on the driveway letting the previous choked back heaving sobs, go.

What would I do without my father?

CHAPTER ONE

A chat with Dad!

This week has been extremely sullen for me since my dearest, loving father left this life last Monday.

Today, the first Sunday, August 26th, 2012, without my wonderful father, I woke with such melancholy, knowing I'd never have the privilege of seeing my father smile, hear his precious voice or ever hug his physical body again. My heart aches for his touch, his embrace, his fabulous wisdom.

The memorial of his life took place last evening, Saturday, August 25th. As I walked into the church of my youth, many came over to pay their condolences. The church probably had seating for 150 or so, and most seats began to fill up.

I sat in the second row with three of my four children and their mates. My eldest son in California, glad he'd spoken to papa that final time and wished he could have made it back home. I knew and know he couldn't change anything and told him *no worries, papa knows how much you love him.*

The Jehovah's Witness religion caused many divisions between all families. Years before, in 1990, I left it, which allowed me to broaden my knowledge of the world beyond the confines of its teachings and its walls.

Newfound freedom opened up for me, almost daily a new way of living and thinking flooded my being. The word metaphysics was now a part of my day to day lingo. I am free from the male based tyranny of this antiquated cult.

As I, and many sat waiting for the speaker to begin, I felt a sense of knowing that a higher energy carried me through this dense fog of pensiveness. However, there was also a definite sense of knowing that all these do-gooders, people I grew up with surrounding me, from within these religious walls, yearned to re-teach me their beliefs. I would never let that happen to me again!

This religion encapsulated each one of us so much so that my father became the overseer for somewhere between twenty and thirty-years, I lost count.

I had been a preacher's daughter. I wanted to talk about my father, however in that religion; women still to this day are not allowed to speak from the platform, facing the audience. Thus, I thought, I'd stand at my seat, turn around and tell the crowd about the man no one really knew, even though they all called him their brother. He was not! He was my father and my sibling's father, never their brother!

When the speaker began his talk of my father, it seemed as though he looked straight at me to say William Victor Gray loved, loved, loved all his babies. He called his children his babies and oh how he loved them all. I fell apart. I tried to hold back the tears; however I lost the battle. I let them roll. Not only did I lose my father, but I also lost one of my very best friends! My daughter, Ashley to my right, hugged my shoulders.

We all lost a great man!

He was the ninth child born to my grandfather Theodore and Grandmother Fidella Gray, living and working on farms the first seventeen years of his life. Grandmother Fidella died when dad was almost five years old. Thus grandfather and dad farmed hundreds of acres alone down in Vienna and Jefferson City, Missouri, utilizing donkeys and horses on a daily basis. The bond between the two grew daily as did my bond with dad.

What would my days be like without chatting with dad? Who'd make silly noises like a donkey, a noise he made with his thumb and forefinger placed strategically on his lower lip, pulled out to make the sound of a jack ass? Who could replace him? No one did it like dad, and we all tried! Dad told us many a day that the donkey's made a noise of which he'd promptly mimic.

Thus today, the first Sunday without my father, I decided that death would not keep us apart! Since I've read countless books, attended meditation and metaphysics classes about life after life and the fact that many meditate to speak with those on the other side; I knew I could do it too!

The rain last night and the sun today seemed to create a calm, a sense of peace that lingered, almost haunting me with calm today. Maybe it was melancholy about what to do without my dad or something more. Should I begin today? Should I try to connect with dad wherever he may be?

The house empty, all kids out and about. Yes, today's the day! I will ask dad questions to see if he responds.

The time 5:14 p.m., I decided to sit on the chaise lounge in the parlor, feet up to relax, my computer on my lap to take notes if anything at all transpired.

I closed my eyes telling self to relax from head to toe, like I've done several times before when meditating for past life regression sessions.

After about ten minutes, I began. "Dad, I'm sitting here viewing your copper embossed 10"x10"x 5" entombment and wondering, what's it like on the other side? I'll ask a question, and perhaps you can enlighten me as to who is with you."

My initial V represents me and D is for dad. With each added session, I've added other names of those I called upon or who wanted to speak with me. I've created a page of the abbreviations at the end of the book.

V: *Have you seen Debbie yet?*

D: *Yes honey, Debbie's right beside me. It's so different here on the other side than when I was on earth.*

V: *How so?*

D: *Well, when I was there with you, I was taught all those years we go on to a Paradise. But now I realize that's false.*

V: *False?*

D: *Yes, I said false. All those years of telling thousands of people we would live in Paradise were false! I wish I'd stayed out of the `truth' like you, Dwayne, Jay, and Penny.*

You see, honey there are throngs of people already here. It's amazing! I've seen my loved ones in this spiritual life and they tell me I'm to encourage other spirits to enlist, yes enlist to go to earth as a physical being to see what that's like. But you know honey; many don't want to experience that.

V: *Really, why not?*

D: *It's like this, and I'm new at this so bear with me. It's so wonderful here, so peaceful and down there I had to work like the dickens to feed my family. But here there's no physical food, just peace, and serenity that surrounds us. We take in a euphoric type of food that sustains and maintains the spirit. Physical people like you and my other babies have to have physical food to sustain life; here we take it all in.*

V: *Oh, so many don't want to become a physical being because it's a great deal of work?*

D: *Exactly! Debbie's been here since 1997 and has come to know what we were taught was false too.*

V: *Yes, I've known that for years. Those false teachings are why the four of us left what the Jehovah Witnesses call* **the Truth,** *because it's not the truth.*

D: *Yes, I saw my memorial and honey, Mr. Chandler, yes I say Mr. because he was not my brother. I realize that now. But he did give a good speech, and was kind when he spoke of me and he was right on when he said I love, love, love my babies.*

What a wonderful experience it was to have known you and my other children, each one, a perfect specimen, to teach me. When a spirit takes on a physical being, we learn things that aren't accessible to us without a transformation.

V: *I've read many books about life after life and wondered about the truth in them. Dad?*

D: *Yes, honey.*

V: *When you were in the hospital on a high from morphine, you were talking out of your head, and it scared us since we never heard you act like that. But during that bit of time perhaps 45-minutes, at one moment in time, you looked up to the ceiling and said ...it's so much bigger than we thought there are so many people there. Jay, Dwayne and I heard you say that and perhaps others. But Dwayne, Jay and I spoke of it afterward. Were you seeing the other side?*

D: *Yes, I certainly did. I saw throngs of people. It was different than what I learned all those years in the religion. Now, I don't claim to know it all because I just arrived but your sister Debbie knows a great deal. Do you want her to explain it?*

V: *Sure, I'd love it. Hi Debbie, I've missed you.*

Deb: *Hi sis, me too. It's so much more than what the religion taught us. At first, it scared me in that many were so kind and we were instructed not to talk to those who weren't part of the religion. However, speaking to others is so poignant because each time we learn a new perspective. Yes, it's just like living on the earth, but so different. When I arrived, I saw Grandma Clark. You know already she exuded kindness at every turn.*

V: *Yes, she was a beacon of kindness.*

Deb: *Indeed. Because of her physical experience, she's very instrumental in teaching those who enlist to have a physical experience.*

V: *Like what?*

Deb: *For instance, when on earth we run into bullies. What should we do when we encounter them? We're taught on earth to fight back, but in reality, kindness is the key. Many physical beings are turned around via kindness and consideration. Our Grandpa Clark was cruel towards grandma, however, because she knew how to deal with him with common sense and compassion she made things work out. Now he was still verbally cruel, but he saw sweetness in her. No, grandpa didn't change, but deep inside, he knew the difference between a kind woman like her and a mean one. So he chose to stay with her. He's here too, to teach. But back to grandma, here her kindness streams to the masses and the children love to see her coming.*

Don't get me wrong, all here are very kind. But because we choose to live different lives and come in through particular mothers and fathers, we then learn diverse relationship energies.

What I mean by that is similar to this example. In an earthly relationship often two people come together to procreate and after the creation is born the two people go their separate ways. In that relationship on earth, the purpose was to create a particular spiritual being to learn various lessons, thus carrying the lessons back to us. Now you might say in that relationship the two people involved were hurt over the breakup. Yes, maybe or maybe not. Both parties came together because this spirit life had to go forth whether it caused a bit grief or hurt between them or not. They didn't know this life experience was also part of their spirits longing to feel and learn what it was like to be, so to speak, in someone else's shoes. Do you understand?

V: *Yes, I see what you mean. Living on earth enables lessons for the afterlife or the spiritual life. Thus from these lessons, it allows new spirit beings to choose what type of parent they wish to be birthed from, right?*

Deb: *Yes, that's it. If we as spirits only take on a parent as we did with dad, we won't know anything but the good.*

Dad: *Well, Debbie, I wasn't all good. I had my very imperfect times. Like in the Navy when I met various women in a variety of ports of call.*

Deb: *Yes, but then that's a lesson you had to learn. See dad; you will be invited to teach others here, the newly enlisted ones what it was like. Yes, many came before us that experienced like situations; however, no circumstance is ever the same.*

Dad: *Hmm, I see, I think. But I did a lot of fighting as well. What can someone learn from that?*

Deb: *Dad, think about it, in your case you didn't go after the fight. You were there to protect your friends or help someone from being bullied, right?*

Dad: *Well, yes I was, although I did think I was kind of cocky.*

Deb: *Perhaps, but then that's the experience you chose. Does that make sense? You were given a lesson to learn the aspects of fighting to help others, thus teaching them to help others.*

Dad: *I guess, but when I turned religious I felt awful that I'd fought at all.*

Deb: *Dad, the religion taught you to think that way. That religion wanted everyone to be as perfect as they could, in a physical body, but how foolish such a line of thinking is. Trying to mold, make or demand a person to be humanly perfect is just something that has never happened, as humans living day to day with other imperfect humans can't possibly create a faultless person. We all chose to be in those bodies to see what it was like as a human being. Not to become perfect.*

The fact is that religion came from an imperfect man who veered off from a religious belief of which he no longer felt suited his purpose. Then he almost demanded his followers to become perfect, which is impossible. His name is Russell who became known as Pastor Russell. Why did he beget that title? It's because he gave himself that grand level of authority. If that religion or any other is all knowing then why are there so many religions? I ask that facetiously. How can a religion be the only true religion when a man formed it? God, as those on earth call the energy that is, didn't profess Mr. Russell would come along two thousand years after Christ. Nor was it stated, he would be the only man to follow and that his words were the only words deemed righteous. No, the energy that is, never spoke of a man named Russell.

Dad: Honey, I think the religion Jehovah's Witness was a great religion as far as religions are concerned. In that, they never fought amongst themselves as the other religions do in war times. But just within these few days of being away from it, I can see how odd it was for me as a human to follow along with his thoughts.

I was devoted to that line of thinking. I do believe the religion kept me from harm in so many ways. I never smoked nor drank in excess because of thinking as they did.

V: Yes, I've often stated the principals are excellent.

Dad: They are. But don't forget where the religion began. It began with a man's thoughts. Yes, he claimed it was from the Bible. But we know mere men wrote the Bible and then called it the greatest book the world has ever known. Why did one book become so famous?

V: I think it's because people as a whole want something to believe in. The Bible became a holy book passed down through the generations, which enabled the masses to have something tangible to hold on to.

Deb: Yes, that's true. Now think about this. This all-powerful book, the Bible, written by many authors, compiled as one book has led so many into separation from one another. Down on earth as a little girl, we were taught the books of the bible as if it was the best thing to know in the world. No offense dad, but now you know that one book can't possibly be the end all to all there is, right?

Dad: Yes, I've come to witness that in a short time. It's like a miraculous transformation upon arriving. I knew without question, all my time on earth; I was there to learn. I'm just glad I decided on the body I selected and my children chose to come through me and mom. What a blessing it was to have and know my precious babies. Within these few days Bixby, there's such a feeling of calm all around, you wouldn't believe how kind and generous our maker indeed is.

V: I can only imagine. I'd like to gain more knowledge of the creator. Is it a he or she? Or is it just a spiritual being neither male nor female as we know?

Dad: Debbie will have to answer that one.

Deb: Yes, we'll cover that as time allows, but back to grandma's teachings in kindness and humility. Remember how she had to deal with our grandpa George?

V: Yes, I do. Dad told me a bit more when here, than what I saw as a child.

Deb: *Well, because grandma lived with a person like him, she's able to explain that type of behavior to the enlisted ones.*

V: *I want to know more about the enlisted ones too.*

Deb: *All in due time. Humility, what does that mean to you?*

V: *Well, it means to lower one's self-boastfulness.*

Deb: *Yes, but it means so much more. Like ...*

V: *I'm kind of tired and think I'll stop this session, ok dad?*

Dad: *Sure, but talk to me again.*

V: *I will. Love you both. Hey I want to know about Grandfather Theodore and Grandmother Fidella, their fathers and mothers, sister's brothers. So many things I'll ask you next time.*

Love you. Dad, you were the best father we could have ever chosen. Till then.

Dad: *Till then.*

This session ended at 5:56 p.m. Short, yes, however, I gleaned a great deal. I discovered that what we believe on earth is entirely or almost entirely wrong. Humans want everyone to think as they do, which causes vast splits and wars. I also, learned that I could converse with my sister and perhaps others, in due time. What a treat!

Also, I noticed I tired rather quickly and all I did was ask a few questions to receive answers.

I sat there in the stillness of thought. What did I just type? Was it readable? I couldn't recall anything I just typed. Is that because I didn't make it up? I knew it wasn't from my imagination of thought. If it were, surely I'd remember at least one sentence, but I couldn't recall anything without reading it. Thus, I read what I'd written, which included misspelled words because I sat there with my eyes shut, in the moment, listening and typing. Much to my amazement dad and Debbie actually told me our religious upbringing was in fact untrue! What a revelation from both of them!

Dad and Debbie were extremely ingrained in that line of thought. I, on the other hand, took what I learned with a grain of salt. Not really believing it nor defending it. I never liked the thinking in that sect that they were somehow superior to others. I knew otherwise.

How did I know this? I think it's because it never got into my bones, as they say. I attended the church with my family, all five meetings each week, with no regrets. I had no problem following my father's lead who became the overseer of the congregation. I thought he was great at what he did, as did the members. But I never let it seep in like some of my siblings. It just wasn't my cup of tea.

I decided when my second husband, an elder in the church, died just three-and-a-half-years into our marriage, that I'd leave the church, with my four children to start a new beginning of freedom of thought, which was a decision well made. The kids' ages, all under fourteen down to fourteen months when he died, had no problem changing with me. The reason it pleased me so, is because with freedom of thought came freedom of enlightenment. I read everything on metaphysics that crossed my path, even attending a weekend retreat at the School of Metaphysics headquarters in Windyville, MO.

I felt I grew up starving for something more. When I left that religion, I felt a wholeness encompass my being. Now new thoughts merged and thankfully brought me to this day where I no longer feel it evil to meditate (like the religion taught) or even to talk to dad or anyone on the other side! What a privilege!

I know, for a fact I will, without a doubt, talk to dad again. I can hardly believe he came to me! I'm thrilled with the astounding fact that there is something more, something beyond our physical bodies and thoughts.

So sweet, my father is still with me!

CHAPTER TWO

Freedoms importance to me

My second and last husband died when I was thirty-six, with four children and no life insurance. Even though my husband recently died, the elders wasted no time taunting me. Within eighteen days of my husband's death, an elder called me asking for the elder books my husband supposedly had. I told him I never heard of them and hadn't looked through my husband's belongings because it was just too soon.

He insisted I give the elder booklets back. I said "Sir, when I have time between four children, meetings and service; I will see if I can find them."

The nerve of those men pushing me around! I made sure I went through my husband's effects finding a few booklets representing the ⁱ**secret elder books**. I read through them noting instructions and realized I could copy them despite their insistence of secrecy. Hence, one day soon after and before the next Sunday meeting when I returned them, I went to the print shop and made copies. While there I kept looking out the window worried an elder might catch me copying those darn books they deemed so necessary to them. Isn't that ludicrous? I felt like a criminal!

The following Sunday, that same elder stopped me as my four children and I entered the church asking if I had the booklets. Again, I was not pleased. Like always, I'd taken my time to bath the babies and the other children the night before, and I made sure all our clothes were clean and tidy too for church the next morning. Something, I'm sure this married elder never had to worry about. This morning I made breakfast for one and all and arrived twenty minutes before the darn meeting began at 10 a.m.!

I handed my baby girl of fifteen-months to my eldest daughter, then fourteen, who knew of the nonsense, telling her I needed to get something from the car. When I left my car, standing by the entrance was the elder who insisted I find the booklets and give them back. He said "I don't see why it's such a problem; sister O gave me her husband's books before two weeks were up. But this has taken you twenty-days." Mind you she was seventy-ish at the time, no small children to deal with after her husband died a few days after mine. Of course, she had no problem giving the books to him because she had little else to do!

I thought it rude to bother me at such a delicate time! I pushed the booklets into his gut and said, "Don't you ever hassle me again, about anything!"

I went inside, sat with my children, listened to the nonsense while thinking; soon I will not come back!

All this during March of 1989; the month my husband passed.

Because of this, the elders in the cult decided I needed a shepherding call. Elder visits consisted of three elders visiting my home shortly thereafter, and one called himself the Traveling Overseer.

I never liked the shepherding calls because they acted with a superior air, somehow better than the congregation members.

I think it may have been about two months after my husband's death when the do-gooder elders emerged on the front porch. As a duteous woman, I greeted them with a smile all the while hating the stupid visit. Because I, a lowly woman lost her husband, I certainly had to be dealt with, so they believed.

After portending concern about my welfare, one of the elders said this to me, "Since you're single now and pretty, we're worried you might jump a man's bones and get into trouble."

"What are you talking about? I've never done anything like that! How dare you assume that because I'm pretty, you automatically think I'm going to bar hop or something like that? I've never done that before and don't even like that idea! I think you're overstepping your boundaries! Shepherding should be a call to see if I need help with anything. Like the roof in need of repair or the plumbing, but you're here to condemn me for being single!"

Then the little short stumpy traveling overseer started with; "We know to own a home alone, might be challenging. We believe you should sell your home and buy a trailer so you can pioneer."

Pioneering in that cult, at that time, was giving up **one-hundred hours per month** as a volunteer to preach *the truth* as their books and magazines profess members should do. That in itself would mean my income would almost cease and I'd more than likely, in their small minds, clean houses to make ends meet like many do in that church.

Funny, those elders never helped me and my first husband out financially when he had nine nervous breakdowns and lost two to three months wages each year. Nor did they ever offer to help me out when my first husband left the cult and left me with two children. Not one of them ever provided a penny or even a bag of groceries! Now, they wanted to tell me to sell my beautiful home, which was the nicest of all the homes the members had at that time.

"Do you? Why do you think that would be better? Don't you realize a trailer depreciates? So you think I should sell this lovely home I worked for, to live in a trailer and lose money. I'll certainly not concede to that. When you pay my bills, then you can tell me what to do! I think you need to leave now."

The little traveling overseer became huffy with me saying, "You're a shark woman!"

"Am I? So you're resorting to name calling. Perhaps you'd like it better if I said yes to whatever you think is best for me. Well, I won't sell my home. I have four children to take care for, and I will take care of them! I have never shirked my responsibilities, and I won't begin now. You've overstepped boundaries and can leave."

I walked to the front door, opened it and out they went.

Goodness, what did I do? I basically threw out those stupid men. I could be kicked out, disfellowshipped for possibly showing disrespect to them and yet what did that little man know of raising a family? He and other traveling overseers aren't to have families nor do those at the headquarters of Jehovah's Witnesses have children.

But they are the ones telling the members how to raise great kids. How can anyone really know until they do it?

I've never been a burden to anyone at that church! Just because I was cute, they automatically accused me of probably jumping the next man's bones! How dare they!

One day that summer, the elders poked their nose into another matter. There was a single man that needed work at the church and knew the art of landscaping; of which I needed help. Since my sons were too young to help me, I offered him the job. He must have told the elders who jumped on me with another shepherding call. I could have helped a fellow member earn a small portion of his living that year. However, they told me I couldn't hire him nor could he take the job. That poor man had been a computer techie back in the day earning $42,000 per year. When he became a baptized JW, he like many, quit their great jobs to pioneer and clean houses losing all they had. It was awful!

I left the cult November of 1989, following nine months of harassment from the elders.

I found in this split, new freedom, no longer worried about elders in their looking glass spying on me or my family. I could now read other books, taboo in that cult, that had an invisible X marked on their cover; the X meaning do not read.

I was free!

The fantastic freedom that ensued unfurled a host of ways to support my babies and live a more fulfilled life.

No longer afraid to read anything other than Jehovah's Witness information, the world opened its loving arms to enable me to realize dreams hidden deep inside. I bought books and or picked up books at the library concerning business, reading three books per week before the kids woke each morning.

I attended numerous business seminars, freely and openly. Oh my, this might have been, at least partially, how the Suffragettes' felt when they gained the right to vote. Of course, they forged ahead to what women *today* call freedom.

Free to think.

Free to breathe!

I was no longer held back by the antiquated elders or the beliefs that hold them captive.

This new freedom is a major reason *why* I ask various questions of that religion throughout the chats with my father.

CHAPTER THREE

Angels among us!

I could no longer wait to chat with dad. I sat my earthly business on the proverbial shelf today Sunday, September 02, 2012 and began again. Noon came, no one home, again I carried my computer to the parlor for our one on one chat. Little did I know what would happen next!

V: *Dad, I wonder if you can visit with me again, to answer a few more questions.*

Dad: *Sure, now I always have time.*

V: *I'm so pleased to have these precious moments in time to talk to you even though you're on the other side. How's this week been?*

Dad: *Honey, it's so different from my earthly experience. You know Debbie told you about Grandma Clark, about how kind she's always been?*

V: Yes.

Dad: *I knew the first time I met her she was a kind soul, and here she continues to help others just like she did when on earth. Her earthly husband George doesn't bother me here like he did on earth.*

V: *How so?*

Dad: *Well honey, he's changed. He went onto the earthly field, so to speak, with a hunger for the type of life he led, which was one of little work, carousing and such. Perk, as I called your grandmother, was the one he leaned on because she desired to fulfill that type of lesson too. She enlisted to become the daughter of her parents to learn that sort of experience.*

V: *Hmm, I see. So she learned what she learned to help others on the other side when she returned. Is that what you mean?*

Dad: *Right. She, like all that enlist to become a physical being; take on lessons at various times in history, to return to this side, which enables others to learn from them.*

V: *How interesting.*

Dad: *I experienced what it was like to live with a woman like your mother. She was cold it's true, but she was also kind. I'm not making any excuses for her behavior because she enlisted just like everyone else to learn that type of connection with me and all our children. Her anger and curtness throughout her life with our kids and others had to have come from the lessons she learned while becoming a child of her parents. Do you notice how that works?*

V: *Of course I do. So that means I came here to learn from that type of a person. You know dad I learned not to treat my children with disdain like our mother treated us, but to teach them to be kind and yet firm in their relationships and to help others. I've always felt I'm here to help others. But I'm not sure how I've helped them, exactly.*

Dad: *Honey, the way you give of yourself when someone needs help that in itself is part of your gift. You're teaching by action, how to give of one's self.*

V: *And you did the same. You were always available to help all those from the church besides your family. Dad, I might add you did a great job of teaching us to give and show kindness to others. Mom didn't know how to teach us that. She did help guide us to be clean and get jobs done on time. Does time matter at all where you are?*

Dad: *No, not at all. We don't even sleep. Oh, we could if we chose to, but there's no need. We don't have a physical body like you that needs constant nourishment with food and sleep. Here we are always learning how to become an enlisted one.*

V: *That word again…enlisted ones. How many are there, on a regular basis, wanting to become human beings?*

Dad: *The word used here is throngs. Throngs of spirits enlist almost like when I enlisted in the service. There are long lines of spirits that wait in* **lines of knowing** *they are to enlist; not a physical line like you know, but a mental line, of a sort. They know when it's time and intuitively are drawn to where they need to be at the moment before they're taught the lessons necessary to become a physical being.*

V: *So, it's a silent knowing of where to be at a particular time or space?*

Dad: *Yes, that's it, a place in time. Each spirit knows without having to be told a time, they just know.*

V: *So, what have you done since last we spoke?*

Dad: *I've hung around with my father and mother, Debbie and oh Tessie and all my siblings are here too. It's like the family reunions we had back on earth.*

V: *Do they sing songs there? Remember you stated your brother Elzie, Evert and the girls sang in harmony here. Do they do that there?*

Dad: *Honey, there's such a sense of peace here that allows all kinds of songs. But yes, my siblings and I sing songs whenever we want. Oh, honey my mom Fidella, is here right now do you want to talk to her?*

V: *Oh my goodness, yes, hi Grandmother. I've heard so much about you from dad. I want to know so much more.*

F: *Hello my granddaughter. I will call you Vickie, okay?*

V: *Sure. I wish I'd met you at least once.*

F: *But you have. I've been there often when you needed help.* (This is choking me up.)

V: *Like when?*

F: *When you and Debbie were in your car and the brakes failed you. Remember?*

V: *Oh yes. I felt an Angel grab the steering wheel at that precise moment and turned it into a massive pile of rocks, so Debbie and I wouldn't go off the embankment. Was that you?*

F: *Yes, dear it was. You had and have so much more to do in that life. That was the only place available I saw that wouldn't hurt the two of you and allow you to walk home to your dad.*

V: *Yes, I recall. When I told dad the steering wheel had been jerked from my hands, he immediately said it had to be the Angels watching out for my babies. And so it was you?*

F: *Yes, and when you were shocked three years before that while doing dishes at age fourteen. Your hands damp with water, you turned the metal upright floor fan to move the air straight onto you as it was a sweltering August day. Plus you* placed your damp right hand onto a metal drawer handle to put silverware in the drawer. I was there. Your mother came running from the bathtub with only a towel to cover her and tripped on the fan cord, which stopped the current from shocking you further.

V: Oh my. I had no idea an Angel was involved then! You know I yelled at the top of my lungs for someone to help me and yet in the yelling, I felt I was whispering like a very soft crying out. However, the neighbor lady heard me, and her house is at least one hundred yards or more away from our kitchen.

F: I hurried your mother to quickly dry off and run into the cord thus causing it to unplug. Both of you could have been shocked to death, had the cord not unplugged.

V: Oh yes, I've gone over that scenario endless times. How miraculous it was for that to happen. But you know what grandmother?

F: What dear?

V: Ever since that moment in time, I've felt a connection to something beyond the earthly realm. But I held back when I thought someone was about to say something that I already knew what they were to say, I held back from stating it, and they blurted out what I thought. To me, it was the beginning of noting my intuitive side.

F: *Yes, dear often it's a trauma like that, which enables the ability to intuit.*

V: *Were you the angel that came when I fell on the ice about ten years ago?*

F: *No, honey that was your grandfather. I was tending to something else here.*

V: *Grandfather?*

F: *Yes, it was your grandfather Theodore.*

V: *Is he there for me to ask a question?*

F: *Yes, dear.*

T: *Hello. It's been a long time since we met. You were only seven when I left that life. Yes, it was me that came to you that day when you fell while ice skating.*

V: *Grandfather, I'm so pleased to know this. When I fell, immediately a man in a tan suede leather jacket and jeans came over to me. Immediately, and I mean immediately he reached with his right hand from my left side to the back of my head and said No, she's not bleeding, she'll be okay. When he placed his hand under my hair, the feeling was so odd in that it felt like he sealed something shut or blended the skull back together. It sounds weird, and yet that's what transpired. His hand also felt like an Angel and a doctor at the same time. It really did! I felt like I was healed all at one moment.*

That fall was so loud that everyone stopped skating. Another man came over to my right, a young man, asking me if he could help me off the ice. I stayed a bit as others quickly surrounded me. But that one man to my left disappeared when all those people came to my aide. Of course, my daughter came over to help me. That fall was odd in that when I fell; I fell onto my rear but also my head fell back and hit the ice with a crack. I thought I split my head open and yet nothing, no headache, no blood, just stunned. When I stood with the help of the young man and my daughter Ashley, I looked around for the man in the tan leather jacket but I didn't see him. I told my daughter to please find that man, to thank him. He was an Angel, I felt, and here it was you, my grandfather.

T: *Yes, dear you looked at every person as they left the rink. But I knew there was no need to stay. You were okay.*

V: *But I was sitting at the only door where people left and I watched the restroom doors across the way, too. No one fit that description. It was odd because I knew that man helped me. I even went back into the rink area when all were off the ice, just after the session ended. I asked the people working if there was another way out. One man pointed to the glass doors chained together on the outer wall and said they're locked but the front doors are unlocked. I sat near the only open door between the rink and the lobby, with ice on my head.*

I knew then and there it wasn't my imagination, but an Angel that came to my rescue. And all along it was my precious grandfather, Theodore.

T: *I was glad to help. You have much more to accomplish in this earthly life.*

V: *Like what?*

T: *Like the book you're writing right now.*

V: *Is it really to be a book?*

T: *Well, dear you already know that, right?*

V: *Yes, I thought so last week when I spoke to dad. When I read last week's journaling to my eldest daughter Rachel, she immediately stated, Mom that's another book. It will help people.*

T: *She's correct. You've already helped her and a few others with the information you've shared.*

V: *True, when I read it recently to two lady friends, the first one called back the next day, her voice stronger than, and not as distressed as the day before. She told me that somehow the reading helped her have hope about meeting her mother on the other side and that she wants to know about her favorite pet. I think the name is Scooter, will she meet up with him?*

T: Oh Yes, if a human has strong feelings for a pet they will certainly meet them here. There are lots of special pets here. No, they aren't here to teach like the former human beings. However, in their silent manners, they do teach spirits and humans alike to be more caring. Yes, she'll be reunited with her Scooter.

V: She'll be pleased to know that. She's mourned him and her parents so much.

T: Who are her parents?

V: The Stockton's, Dorthea and James. Do you know them?

T: I know they're here; however I don't know them personally. I have so many from my family and friends here that we, like when on earth, stay connected to those we know well. Of course, we have large meetings at times to hear what transpired on the other side.

V: Really, like what?

T: Each time we have, say fifty spirits come forth, which of course is ongoing, we have a meeting of the minds. In that, we automatically know what their experiences were. Well, sort of, then we have meetings that might take hours in your time, but in ours, it's a meeting of explanations of how this or that type of human lived out their lives, but it takes only moments to hear, if you will, what was learned.

V: *How amazing. So a meeting of many will take moments in time because you're all so in tune with one another? Is that it?*

T: *Yes, sort of. It's hard to explain.*

Dad: *Honey, it's like a silent knowing. Like you mentioned you knew an angel healed and or helped you when you fell on the ice. It's like that, which is very quick.*

V: *Oh, I see. Yes, it is swift. A knowing from within of what is.*

Dad: *Exactly!*

V: *Again, I've learned so much more. Thank you. I will contact you again. Funny how this tires me so much, however at the same time I'm also rejuvenated! Thank you one and all for this enlightenment.*

Dad, I'll call upon you soon. Love you as always you're little Bixby.

Dad: *I came up with that nickname when you were a little one. I think I heard a movie star with that name or something like that and it stuck.*

V: *I've always loved the endearing nickname. Love to you all. Talk soon.*

Dad: *Grandfather and grandmother, love you too.* {It's 1 pm}

Note: I keep my eyes closed when I channel. My words are misspelled a bit because I try to type as fast as I receive the information, which allows no site interruptions.

CHAPTER FOUR

A silent knowing

When I woke late this Sunday morn, September 16th, 2012, (8:38 a.m. is late for me) I thought I must chat with my father. Refreshed from a great night's sleep, I showered and realized my youngest two adult kids were out and about. Ah, the perfect time to chat with dad.

V: *Hello Dad, it's your Bixby. What have you experienced lately?*

Dad: *Well, honey I've had such a great time with my family and learning things I never thought possible on the earthly realm.*

V: *Like what?*

Dad: *Like learning that all are one and the same in the site of God, the Universe, or whatever anyone on earth deems the energy that **is**; is the all-powerful energy, which created our planet and the masses of planets that stream the many galaxies.*

V: *What is the energy actually called where you are?*

Dad: *Honey it's almost a consensus that the energy is sort of a silent knowing, a knowing that all exist because of this energy. I know that doesn't explain the energy; so let me say this, there are no pearly gates to enter. There's just a crossing over to a brighter more knowledgeable side of things. It's a very pleasant feeling, being here.*

V: *Where's here?*

Dad: *It's just a different space, there's no up here and down there, it's just a being place. Yes, that's it. A being place of knowledge. The energy is the knowledge that we all have but on earth are blocked, because of the vast array of people's ideas pulling each one in many directions. Like the great masters throughout time, those men and women saw beyond what all, or the masses see while on earth. They saw a different thought process, which enabled them to speak to the masses either on a platform like Patrick Henry or in a book of verse. No one person on earth who spoke on those platforms saw things as the masses did and do. They gave talks to help the masses see beyond what **is** on earth. Earth is just a place to learn for the afterlife. It's an experience that spirits choose to enlist into and inhabit. There's a saying on earth that the enlightened ones say, we are not human beings having a spiritual experience but are spiritual beings having an earthly experience.*

V: *I see, so persons here on earth that seem to have some specialized knowledge to share with us, these, I guess, have* carried over perhaps thoughts from their spiritual life? Is that it?

Dad: *Sort of, but few adults recall anything from here. However, little ones always do; although, they can't speak of it until they know how to talk and by that time they're indoctrinated by their parents who were indoctrinated by their parents. The parents, all well and good, try to teach the children what they know and what they learned. Do you understand why so many live their lives in one religion because that's what they were taught?*

V: *Yes, I see.*

Dad: *If one and all would open their minds to hear what others say, they would have a much better existence on earth.*

V: *How do you mean?*

Dad: *If they were open-minded they would understand others thoughts better and their new ideas.*

{Interrupted, the computer froze! The session ended here 10:31 a.m.}

CHAPTER FIVE

Children born on earth

Today, is a sunny and chilly Saturday, September 22, 2012, 9:14 a.m. Many days like this I might have picked up dad, and driven him to his hometown in Vienna, MO while listening to tales of his childhood. However, the book I wrote of his life titled The Ankle Express - Life and Times of William Victor Gray (2012), will have to suffice from now on. Or of course, a mental transference session is in order, like author William Atkinson wrote of and noted in his book, Practical Mental Influence, and Mental Fascination. (1908)

Therefore, I reread the previous session and will see if we can continue. I'd love to know more.

V: *Dad, its Bixby again. Are you there?*

Dad: *Yes, honey. How are you?*

V: *I'm okay at this time. I wonder if we could continue our talk from last week.*

Dad: *Sure.*

V: I've just reread my notes and wonder about the children born here. You stated many of 'those in the know,' have said that the little ones know more than they can tell us because they can't speak until after a year or more, which is after their parents have indoctrinated them. In turn, parents teach them what they've learned about life, religion etc. right?

Dad: Yes, when I was there learning, I had no idea that the religion was false. I'd been taught to be a good person by both my parents, mother a short time and father the rest of his life. He was a Methodist later in life and a Nazarene when I was young, but most of the family Baptist. Now what all don't realize on earth, is that the different religions that fight over their beliefs are merely fighting over one book called the Bible that they interpret their way. Just like the Jehovah's Witness religion that I became a member of, sometime in 1954. Remember honey those kind people the Plunkett's?

V: Yes.

Dad: They were very kind to me, and I thought what they taught was correct. I later learned and now realize it is their kindness that enables others to change their thoughts to believe as they do. There's no difference in any religion except when one is ready to change their mind and a preacher or whoever knocks at their door, so to speak, they are ready for a change. It's no big epiphany; it's just that they are ready for a change.

V: *Hmmm, so when my siblings and I were ready for a change, we wouldn't have been treated so poorly from those in that religion, had they understood that process.*

Dad: *That's right, and you know honey; I have to apologize for my actions in that. I didn't understand that you had the right to change your mind as I did mine from the Baptist sect to the Jehovah Witness sect. We simply outlive various beliefs.*

V: *Dad even though you were in that religion you still included all of your children as your family members, when we left it. It doesn't excuse the vast array of secrecies that you held because we weren't a part of that cult, but you did show us love at all turns. No exceptions. I liked that. You actually set aside the religion enough to be our father no matter what.*

Dad: *Yes, I hoped I did that.*

V: *You did. Now back to children that come through various parents to see what life is like on earth, can you explain?*

Dad: *Yes, the children. First, you need to know there are no births here as in the earthly realm. But there is a type of birthing here in that those that come back to the spirit realm, are rebirthed, if you will, to spiritual life and we engulf them in love and kindness to help them transition.*

V: *Transition?*

Dad: Yes. It's almost as if they have to shed the cloak of earth and sort of cleanse their being of the drudgeries from earth.

V: Drudgeries?

Dad: Yes, drudgeries. When on earth, earthly beings pick up all the energies of those that surround them. There's a vibration that engulfs each human-being, either for their good or not. Those in prison, are inundated with physical and mental weights, if you will, that pulled them into the state of affairs they got into, which in turn placed them in prison.

Prison on earth is so very miserable because the people succumbed to how they were brought up. IF, and this is a huge word IF, they would have opened their minds to think differently, they may never have been incarcerated and would have been free to see what else earthly life had to offer. But then we wouldn't have learned as much about that type of person when we return here.

V: It is all so fascinating!

Dad: Yes, it is. The children have to be birthed from various types of parents to learn whatever it is they chose to learn by choosing their birth parents.

V: We choose our birth parents? That's incredible! I've read that before wondering of its validity.

Dad: Yes, it is valid and incredible. Just think honey, I chose my birth parents to come to earth precisely when history was changing yet again. My mother, I already knew would leave soon. Oh, on earth I didn't recall anything that she set up while here, but now I remember what had to have transpired because we `know' what we know when here, and choose accordingly before we enlist to go to earth. Oh, honey, it's been such a treat to meet back up with my parents. They were and are such great beings!

V: I'm pleased for you that you're with them. When you have time would you ask grandmother what she or how she felt when here?

Dad: Honey, you can ask her yourself.

V: Right now?

Dad: Sure, we don't go to work as you do, nor are we distracted when one from earth contacts us. We do all we need to do, even while we speak to you.

V: Really, How so?

Dad: Well, I'm speaking to you, and I'm also conversing with my parents, Debbie and others.

V: Really, how do you do that?

Dad: We don't speak with our mouths as humans. We talk with our spiritual minds. It's an all-knowing conversation. With you, I have to form words, so you understand. Here we all speak the same language even though there are former humans from all over the galaxies.

V: So, let's touch on that. Are there beings from other planets that are in the same realm you're in?

Dad: Yes, there are many-many galaxies as you know, but more than any human can imagine. We, as spirits, through our minds, speak.

Just when I had another question to ask, the session abruptly ended at 9:44 a.m.

...

Again, my computer froze!

Since I squeezed in this session before an appointment, I can only believe the Universe, like many, many times prior to this moment in time, chose to freeze my computer. When this happens, it's as if the Universe is there to prod me to do the `other' important thing I must do.

I love to write, read, research, however these gems-in-time cause me to reflect on the grand universal aspects of all we do. Thus, I pay attention.

CHAPTER SIX

A simple cup of tea

On this Monday, September 24th, 2012, dad came to me differently than via channeling meditations.

I must add that several weeks without my dear father is almost too much to bear! Plus, I had a tough time this week with a female client that would not leave her home (as per the contract) for my crew and me to set up her estate sale properly. Each day we left, I thought we finished the setup in a particular room or area and then each morning I went back, only to note she set items on top of what I just organized the day before or all over the walkways! I was swimming upstream, or so I thought only to back-slide each morn when I returned to work. After four and a half days of her interference, I had to cancel the contract. I needed the income but needed my sanity more.

My business is straightforward if the client lets me do it!

That same evening, beaten down from the unruly client and saddened from dad's passing, I made a cup of tea to relax, all the while mentally chattering to Dad of this woman. Then, when I sat the teacup down on my nightstand, and much to my surprise, the foam that's rarely there, after stirring it, read hi.

I snapped this picture immediately!

I knew, in my heart, my father came to comfort me.

I said out loud, "Hi dad, glad you're here! It's been a tough week!"

Equally surprising and just as I sat on the right side of my bed, a gnat made a bee-line towards my face, hitting me smack dab on my right cheek!

"Dad, did you just kiss me?"

Within less than a minute, that gnat came right back at me; slammed into my right cheek again as if to say, "Yes, its dad."

"I love you."

"All will right itself."

"Don't give up."

Well, I haven't given up! Within the next few days and weeks that followed this *teacup* intervention from dad, my estate sale business catapulted from a bit of a skip to a hop every week! We handled one sale per weekend till the end of the year!

My brother Dwayne and I both agreed that we think dad is helping me obtain all the sales, from beyond. I'd like to think so.

CHAPTER SEVEN

Spiritual foot print & Galaxies

Again I've reread the previous information from September 22nd, to inquire further on this particular subject, it's September 28, 2012 6:20 a.m.

V: *Dad, it's me again. Are you there?*

Dad: *Sure honey, I'm always here.*

V: *I just had a thought. What if you decide to enlist into another set of parents? Will I still be able to chat with you as I know you?*

Dad: *Most assuredly, honey, if I choose to enlist that doesn't stop this spirit being you know as your father. But let me assure you further. I need to learn more before I re-enlist which I may or may not do.*

V: *Oh, okay, great. So I can still contact you and know it's you?*

Dad: *Yes, I will always be this spirit even if I re-enlist. I will become yet another spirit but will still have this spirit in my spiritual footprint.*

V: *Spiritual footprint. I like that. Okay, so I wanted to continue our last conversation about other galaxies of beings. Okay?*

Dad: *Of course. The other galaxies have many beings in and amongst them just like we do. How silly it is for humans to think or suppose they are the only chosen ones to have the privilege of life after spirit. The masses that encompass the vast outer space gain knowledge they gather while traveling to planets just like we pick up by visiting earth.*

V: *So do other spirits from those areas enlist to visit earth?*

Dad: *Yes, they do.*

V: *How would we know?*

Dad: *You wouldn't know the differences except that the other spirit energies enlist to visit earth are somewhat out there. They are those on earth that see things vastly different, as if, they are from another planet. Like you've told your brother Dwayne, he must have come from another planet to have such amazing stories resonate through him.*

V: *Yes, I have stated that, but I don't recall ever telling you that.*

Dad: *You probably never did, but as mentioned before, there is a knowing of what is, here. So I picked up on the knowing that you told him that.*

V: *How intriguing.*

Dad: *The knowing that other spirits have; allows some, note I said some, to open up about what they see and hear subconsciously. Possibly by writing a book or they think outside the box and share it with others. That knowing or knowledge has made many a person on earth very wealthy under the umbrella of earth's confines.*

V: *Earth's confines? You mean the wealth is only confined to earth because they can't take it with them?*

Dad: *Exactly. The vast array of riches one accumulates on earth, all the fights that ensue because of a piece of paper called money, are strictly confined to the earth. Conflicts between brothers and sisters, state against state, country against country, ensue to confirm that one particular entity is better than another. It's tragic from here and while I was on earth, I thought it deplorable too. Even though I entered the Great War to fight and never had to, but I would have because on earth there's a fighting state of mind in men, not women. Men think they must be better than the other man; thus fights and wars occur. It's lamenting to now know what I know and wish I knew it when on earth. But the earthly realm is where we receive the energies that are, when and only when we enlist.*

V: *As a woman, I've never understood why men like to fight for this and that. Even as little children, boys struggle at early ages. Oh, girls fight too, but they don't choose or rarely choose to kill someone over what they believe is their consideration of right or wrong. Its' heartbreaking to see and hear about vast killings here and in other countries. To me, it's almost effortless to get along. Sure I have opinions, but it's easy to stay calm and not fight about it and talk it out. Simple.*

Dad: *It is effortless to talk things out. But honey, so many humans want things their way that they don't see the simplicity in talking. They'd rather bully someone to get what they want.*

V: *True, so back to the other galaxies. I need a bit more information. When we read a book that seems odd, like it came from another planet, it probably did?*

Dad: *More than likely, the ones that share that information seamlessly open up thoughts in many to see beyond what's in front of them. They open to another dimension, which in turn allows perhaps some inkling of where they previously were as a spirit. It may even cause them to read more books in that field, which in turn enlightens them further to the possibility of life on other planets.*

V: *So, this of course, makes me think of movies I've seen depicting outer space and spaceships. I've often wondered why the writers even thought of those stories, which intrigue the* masses. And now it has to be because they, the writers, were from other planets. Is it not just their imaginations?

Dad: *Well, yes it is their imaginations based on a subconscious knowledge from their spirit lives. However, they don't realize that, until they come back to the spirit realm.*

V: *So we receive these bits of information, a knowing, from the other side, and we don't even know it! I love it! Thus, the books Dwayne's writing, more than likely come from beyond, and happened in another place in outer space? I'm writing a book titled My Past Life with Henry Ford, which I believe is most definitely a past life connection. Otherwise, how could I have known all the details except without the subconscious coming to the fore?*

Dad: *Yes, more than likely. Now don't get me wrong, writers have vivid imaginations. They certainly are gifted with perceptions from the other side or other planets or whatever you want to call it. But they don't recognize it's from another planet or spirit existence that they are now sharing with the masses on earth.*

V: *Hmm, I love this information! Those that write or speak about things unlike the masses do, and in turn closed minded ones, think they're crazy. When in actuality they aren't crazy, they merely think out of the proverbial box we humans set up as normal, and pay attention to what they receive, right?*

Dad: *Precisely! You got it.*

V: *Now, I have another question. Actually, I have zillions! But this one gnaws at me.*

Dad: *Okay shoot.*

V: *The religion we grew up in professing to be right and as you know they call it **the truth**, which it isn't. But, if it is **the truth** then why do they believe in a paradise? It's almost like they're all children in a dreamland. I never did get that.*

Dad: *Honey, let's take further steps into that thought process. When the first man Russell, who began the Jehovah's Witness sect, decided to drop his beliefs from the Mason belief and create his following, he did it based on the Bible. The Bible was and is something the masses believe in as the saving grace, so to speak from that life. Now, think about this, when Mr. Russell broke off from his former religious beliefs, he did so because he understood the Bible differently, which all read. However, he saw it in a divergent light or perspective, which is what all religious sects do. He knew that to begin on his own, he had to make powerful speeches to sway as many as possible to believe his way. Just changing one's mind doesn't make the masses follow you. But using the **Bible** as the means or the go-between, to sway the masses, works over and over on the earthly realm. Russell saw things vastly different; thus he picked up on a paradisiac system where all is beautiful, clean, no strife; the lamb will lay down with the lion. Think about that statement, the lamb lying down with the lion. You get a visual picture of overall peace, don't you?*

V: *Yes, I do. Almost like lightness is in the air, the sky blue, flowers abundantly surrounding the lamb and lion.*

Dad: *So think about this, the lamb could represent kind, mild ones on earth and the lion, the hard nose men who try to shove things down one's throat even though they don't want to believe that way. What if this paradise that is so sought after in* **the truth**; *what if it's only a way of thinking to keep the masses involved with Mr. Russell and become his followers because there's light at the end of the tunnel or a pot of gold at the end of the rainbow. Both are false. But you see honey, it creates a false sense of security, that If I do this or that a certain way on this earth, then I'm rewarded like a little child with a lollypop.*

V: *So you're saying Mr. Russell pulled thoughts from the Bible that helped him sway persons that needed a pot of gold at the end of the rainbow?*

Dad: *Yes, there are so many that can't seem to find their way on earth unless they have something to hope in. They have to have, if nothing else, a belief that there is something better, just around the corner.*

V: *Well, I like to think there is something more, to be sure. It keeps me going.*

Dad: *Precisely!*

V: Oh I see. If we, on earth, don't have a goal to reach or attain to, then we are basically floating along day to day without cause. Is that it?

Dad: Yes, in a way. These religions create a goal, if you will, for the masses that by believing in that goal, is their salvation or their freedom from life's drudgeries.

V: There's that word again. I don't think I ever heard you speak of drudgeries while here. You always seemed so positive here.

Dad: Yes, because I only saw what my dad taught me and that was to be positive. Dad showed me positivity his entire life. He'd say son, you can either wake in the morning with a smile or a frown. Why not wake happy and go through the day with a smile. You can change what you want when you're happy. Sadness creates mental drudgeries honey; which are a mental state of mind. Going through one's life drudging or carrying the weight of the world on one's shoulders, as opposed to waking happy and positive, is like carrying around a ton of brinks with you every day while on earth. Drudgeries are cleansed when a spirit returns home. They have to have a cleansing to shake off the dense energies that befall humans.

V: I wonder if other planets have these drudgeries.

Dad: Spirits don't expect drudgeries when they enlist on a planet. They go to see what it's like in that living being and then return. They all have to cleanse their spirits when they return. Thus by cleansing, they open the way to share what they just learned. This cleansing begins right when we arrive. I didn't even know it was happening. Again, that mental information like we get when we enlist is similar to the cleansing effect when we first arrive. A certain ethereal calmness seemed to wrap around me, the first few days or maybe it was an entire year, time is not a factor here. But the calm, which is always here, I later learned, is centered on the cleansing upon arrival. There's no special place in the **here**; however it happens just the same.

V: It's all so thought-provoking. I know I keep saying that, but I never knew I would learn so much by talking to you this way. The first time I contacted you, I just wanted to have my father back. Here, you've enlightened me; thus this information may enlighten others too when I correct all the misspelled words and create a book. Funny, dad I can type extremely fast, but when we speak like this I mess up the spellings. Oh, I can decipher the writings no doubt because it's not as dire as it may seem, although some things run together because I get all excited with what you're sharing.

Dad: It's alright. I'd be the same way if I received these messages and I could hardly type like you.

V: It's a wonderful and easy way to communicate, with my eyes closed and no distractions. Of course this day I'm up early, the house quiet before anyone goes to work.

Dad, I think that's all for now. Check with you later, okay? Love you.

Dad: *You can contact me anytime. Oh, and tell Ashley I don't mean to scare her when she sees me in her dreams or just after she wakes. She is very intuitive and needs to recognize she's receiving information from the other side. Tell her to relax at night and to tell the ones that come through not to scare her but give her information she can share with others.*

V: *Ok, I'll tell her. She'll be pleased to know that. She loves you so dad, as do all my babies.*

Dad: *Yes, tell her I felt close to all your children because they didn't have a father. Well, the older two do, but he wasn't there for them like others that don't have a father to guide them. So I felt like I should be there for all of them if ever they needed me. I hope they knew to ask.*

V: *Well, I know Ashley and Rachel asked, and I know Caleb and Blake, as men tried not to ask advice often, but oh my how they all love you. It's been a wonderful trip this life having a father like you. I've said this often, that so many of my friends wished they had a father like you. I wonder if your kindnesses show that you've been here before.*

Dad: *Yes, I've been on the earth before.*

V: *As what or whom?*

Dad: *I was an inventor in most of my lives. That's why I liked to invent so many things in the last life. I never saw to it to share with the masses, but tinkering was a pleasure I sought in all my lives.*

V: *But, would I know any of the names?*

Dad: *Well, maybe.*

V: *Okay, who were you?*

Dad: *One time in space in the 1800's, I was Thomas Evergood. My father was a banker in Maine. I only lived into my teens because pneumonia took me. But I was instrumental at the bank with the locking mechanism in the safe.*

V: *Really? Maybe I can find some research on that. Funny, my hands now feel like I'm typing on a keyboard that is slanted in the shape of a V. An upside down V and it feels like I'm typing all the wrong letters. What is that?*

Dad: *Maybe this session should end. Perhaps you're more tired than you think.*

V: *Maybe. I opened my eyes a few times to make sure my keyboard hadn't changed on me. Of course, I know it hasn't, but it's the weirdest feeling. I will contact you again. Love you.*

Dad: *Love you too and tell all the little ones I love them as well.*

V: *I will, by for now.*

It's 7:37 a.m. One hour – 17 minutes, that's the most extended session yet. Maybe they should only last about an hour, which might lesson how strange my hands feel. We'll see.

What a wonderful session! So much information came forth.

I've searched hours for a Thomas Evergood-inventor and haven't found him yet. I must have misunderstood the name.

CHAPTER EIGHT

Something more

This morning, Sunday, October 14, 2012, 7:14 a.m., in my journal I wrote I've been incredibly somber of late. Thus on October 10th, my daughter Rachel, did a healing session with me for an hour that remarkably lifted the gloominess that day. Not only have I been heartbroken since dad's passing, but my siblings and I have had to deal with our mother's distressing ten-year dementia continuum. Mother, a cold, self-centered woman, unkind to the kids, thus never as delightful as our father, has left me with little feelings good or bad towards her.

Today, a strange occurrence happened while sitting with my laptop and chatting with dad and my sister Debbie, who passed December, 1997. I'd barely begun working on this session when the computer entirely shut off at 7:38 a.m.! It was plugged in, and it just shut off! I'd been communicating with my sister Debbie at the time, and after twenty-four minutes, it shut off and wiped clean. I save once I'm finished with each session because I'm sort of in a trance of listening and typing.

Thus, I had to meditate further, asking my guides and angels to reclaim some of what she told me, and they did, but in small doses.

After a short time, they helped me to recall her stating how religious sects, Jehovah's Witnesses and others are only about holding us back from learning something more or stepping out beyond their teachings.

She also stated, when the spirits enlist they choose who to come through based on the parent's beliefs and what the spirits want to learn. However, because these religious sects/cults (she used these words frequently) disable us from learning anything outside their rigid beliefs. These rigid beliefs, in turn, disable spirits to determine what they would like to learn on earth via certain parents.

I can't believe all this information was wiped clean and I did nothing to shut down the computer nor was the power cord unplugged!

I do know that every time I think I have to do something other than what I'm typing, something generally goes awry, like today.

I kept thinking I have to hurry and get ready for an estate sale I'm handling, shower, etc. and arrive by 9:30.

Whoosh!

Simply, wiped clean!

The entire discussion, gone!

I called upon dad first and he said he was fine, I then asked about Debbie's children – how does she feel about the way they behaved when dad was in the hospital. She stated *they are no different than others who are indoctrinated with those cult-like beliefs.* I asked midway *do you think your children will ever leave the cult.*

She stated *we don't tell the future*; however, she said one would leave but would not tell me which one. I believe it will be the son, but time will tell.

Wow, strangely weird to lose all that information.

I feel the spirits or angels are telling me to get ready for my job. It's now 7:48 a.m. and my alarm clock has incessantly chirped since 7:40.

So off I go.

I will address this another time, to be sure!

CHAPTER NINE

Family & Obstacles

Good morning dad, how are you today? I don't know why I keep asking how you are. It's quite silly since I know you're in a loving, peaceful atmosphere.

Another Sunday, October 28, 2012 – 7:44 a.m., grief is atrocious! How does a person ever feel normal again after losing such a special person? Goodness, I abhor loving and letting go!

Dad: *Hi honey, oh, I couldn't be better. You know I've learned so much in these few short weeks.*

V: *Tell me, if it's allowed.*

Dad: *Sure, it's allowed, honey. All those we thought would come out of the memorial tombs in a resurrected physical form will never happen. It's like this, on earth, human beings feel they have to know or have to feel there's a physical resurrection to the earth, when in fact, the actual revelation or transformation is upon arriving back here.*

V: *So you mean the information taught in the Bible is not factual about the resurrection?*

Dad: Correct, all on earth and me included thought we'd go through a war called Armageddon and when we'd make it through alive to the other side; we'd then see our relatives come back to life.

Well, that isn't true.

It is true here on the other side, as some refer to it, that we do see our passed family members and rejoice with great jubilation. No doubt it would be an incredible task to see the dead ones rise out of their tombs or graves; however, it's just not so. That sad to say, is something written by a man or many men and stated that it was a spiritual experience and thus they wrote it.

V: *Well, to me this is a spiritual experience, and I'm writing it. What's the distinction?*

Dad: *The distinction is humans need something to believe in; something to hope for and the Bible became the object to catapult the masses into a specific belief system. Therefore, the belief that all those in the memorial tombs are to rise and come forth isn't a reality. Humankind always wants something or someone to hope in. Thus scholars, when the Bible was written, knew this and offered a hand, so to speak, by encouraging humans to carry on in life because there would be a reason to go further. I see how that could be contradictory.*

It's like this. Life on earth can be very dull if a person doesn't have any goals. In a religion of any kind the followers automatically have goals set for them via the host of preachers etc.

V: *Oh, I see. So the Bible was and is instrumental in helping those who don't or won't set earthly goals to push them into sort of a forward mode?*

Dad: *Yes, of a sort. It's like this; human beings want something more, always have and always will. When I was on earth, I wondered why all are there. What's the purpose? This question like many has puzzled me, and I know your children question it too. They are all seeking something outside a box-like mentality. In that, they subconsciously know this life is a shallow existence and then we die. But for those, not in the box of mental prison, like going to and from church seeking their answers; many young and old have opened up a new-age way of thinking, hence, seeking information on their own. Many have written books on subjects such as life after life, something the religion we were in claimed as false. But honey, it's not. If those that sit in judgment over others would open up and actually see beyond their religious building and beliefs, then all wars would cease.*

V: *How so?*

Dad: *Well, they would cease because all would think alike. Wars are fought generally because of uncompromisable beliefs, which many times are religious beliefs. What those on earth don't understand is that all are spiritual beings having a physical experience. Not the other way around. Many like you, open up to the actual possibility of something more beyond the earthly church beliefs that cause massive divisions.*

Church and State have fought often over religious beliefs. Wars fought overseas note all walks of life and all strains of religious beliefs with many of the same beliefs, but fight one against the other. It's disheartening when Presidents declare war and massive amounts of men join to fight against those of the same faith.

Yes, of course, there are other wars started outside of religious beliefs. At any rate, it's a crying shame war is fought at all. It's effortless to talk things out, but then its men who don't want to be wrong and thus battle begins.

V: *Yes, I know that's true. May we change the subject?*

Dad: *Sure honey, what do you want to know?*

V: *A few weeks ago I was talking with Debbie, do you recall?*

Dad: *Yes, she was telling you about her children.*

V: *Yes, but I wonder if you could enlighten me a bit on that subject?*

Dad: *Sure, shoot.*

V: *You and I know that four of your children left the religion and we are all much more enlightened and think outside that proverbial religious box. Even you left for about eight years.*

Dad: *I did leave the church and you know honey during that time, I was the freest I'd been in years. I wrote my book and many poems that I would never have written. The elders would have thrown their religious texts at me for writing poetry about Christmas or anything for that matter, that wasn't related to their line of thinking.*

V: *Yes, I know. Really, it is a sickness to keep all those in the religion, hands tied, so to speak, without the ability to read and or write something from within or read others information. Thus a disfellowshipping could take place if one was found out.*

It's deplorable, truly deplorable!

But my inquiry is about why Debbie's children and others in the religion claim to be Christians and yet when you were in the hospital, and then at your home, some of her three adult children were very disrespectful to me. I know you taught us to respect our elders. But especially Debbie's youngest has not been trained like that; it troubles me for her future.

Dad: *She like many others in that religion and I was no exception, is taught to respect their elders, but here's the kicker. If non-believers like you and the other kids are involved in a circumstance, the `others' in the religion believe the rules don't apply to outsiders. They think they are the only chosen ones to* carry on their religious beliefs. Since you and I and scores of others left it, then those that left are no longer a viable cog in their religious wheels of beliefs. Does that make sense?

V: Yes, to me it's always been that way. The disrespect has always been a bone of contention with me. I've taught my children to have respect for an older person, no matter what their religious belief system is. They are to respect all elders with equal respect, unless the criminal element is involved, which commands a certain caution.

Dad: Yes honey, Debbie's children learned from a father born of an alcoholic father; thus his beliefs are vastly different than how my father taught me. His views, I now know, are based on what he learned as a child. Thus, all the teachings in the world won't wash away the foundation of instability he grew up with. Don't get me wrong; there's no excuse for any young person to disrespect their elders.

I experienced disrespect with those children too. When I'd help them, they never said thank you, and I thought it very odd. I soon realized where it came from and by finally leaving that life and learning what I now know; I can see even more clearly, where it all came from.

As earthly parents, we have to train our children to respect others.

I know it's been a bone of contention with you. I saw and heard the disrespect. That's why I told you and you alone one day on *my death bed* **that it may be hot or cold, but you'll have to be the one that carries things out.**

V: *I wondered if you meant that statement or if you were incoherent at the time because you were always coherent, to the end. Thus I felt you said it because of the straining circumstances they placed me in.*

Dad: *That's precisely what I meant! You must realize these are human beings who know not what it's like to think as you and I experienced those years away from the cult, to think on a higher plane of thought. Beyond the many books, the cult puts out and into a clearer way of thinking, which promote every new dawn.*

V: *What do you mean, by new dawn?*

Dad: *A new dawn on earth, is a new day. A new start or enlightenment occurs on earth when someone opens to a new line of thinking. This process begins endless aha experiences while on earth, which in turn enables a better and fuller life while there. Thus when the earthly life ends, and we return to our original spiritual being, we then have more to teach others here.*

When we enlist birth into various parents, we then learn what that one life can learn under whatever the circumstances may be. Plus, because the earth evolves within each day and each day brings on new technologies, instruments, books, etc. these items bring on new ways of thinking. Hence new babies born to various parents, during different timeslots on earth, enable a new line of teaching when they leave their earthly bodies. Does that make sense?

V: *Oh yes, totally! That helps me to have more compassion for those that haven't reached the higher level of thinking, and not to judge them. I wonder if, like Debbie stated, in the last very short session that one of her children will leave the cult, I wonder if all will eventually leave it.*

Dad: *Honey, time will tell. All her children may become enlightened, but they will have to play out their experiences to get to that point. It may not take place within their current lifespan.*

V: *Again today has been a very informative experience. I will contact you soon, my sweet father. Please say hello to Debbie and tell her this earthly sister has missed her as far back as the nine years before her death when her husband wouldn't allow us to talk or visit, even though we lived two miles apart.*

Dad: *Oh, she knows, and is much more open to all possibilities. I had the pleasure of leaving the cult for those eight years or so. During which time, I became more and more aware of all the other boundless and endless experiences a person can have, if only humans would open their minds to listen and learn.*

V: *Yes, to me this life is all about listening, reading, researching, asking questions and ultimately gaining* knowledge. Thus this knowledge begets wisdom. I love to learn! Love you dad. Talk soon.

Dad: *Love you too. I'm so thankful you know how to communicate with me.*

V: *Even if I didn't know how I'd figure it out. You're too special not to talk to.*

Till the next chat....

CHAPTER TEN

Dreams-Spirituality-Optimus & Spisterterious

Today is my eldest son, Caleb's birthday, Friday, February 22, 2013, which caused me to think of how unique we all are and the need to chat with my lovely father.

V: *How's my one and only favorite Dad?*

Dad: *Always fine. Hi honey, how are you?*

V: *I'm fine; I wish we could talk in person. But I'll take this just the same. I finally, after these many months, listened to your voice yesterday with tears cascading down my cheeks. But it was good to hear you make the noise like the donkey. Remember?*

Dad: *Yes, of course, I remember. I'd hear the donkeys on the farm; make noises every time we went on a saw-set all around the country. It was fun to make that noise because my dad liked to listen to it and made fun of me.*

V: *Too cute! So what have you been up to these past few months?*

Dad: *I've learned so much, so much more than when on earth.*

V: *I'm sure you have; in what way?*

Dad: *I've learned our spirits sort of hang around and join with those that enlist to come back in human form. And the spirits have lots of lives they carry back from one generation to the next. Like when I used to feel, as a human, that I'd been to one place or another before, we called it déjà vu. Because you see, the spirit that I became before birth to my parents was in that location or a place I traveled to during my last lifetime.*

V: *Exciting. So when I had my dream about Henry Ford and learned that all the dream information was in fact, correct, it came to me because I had lived that life before?*

Dad: *Yes. However, it can mean something else.*

V: *Hmmm. I presume that means that the names and information of Victoria Zane, Charles Currothers, Henry Ford, his house and business buildings I saw in a dream, were because some spirit came to me or I lived it in a previous life?*

Dad: *Yes, a mental vortex opened to allow you that information. But honey, the vortex was from a spirit that knew you were to write a book and gave you the connective information to make it happen. But, now here's the kicker, you actually paid attention to the dream and wrote that novella about it. Most humans have dreams but never and I mean never believe in them, so they don't write them down as you do.*

See, dreams are a very significant part of human life. When humans sleep they don't forget the events of the current day nor do they forget any of their past lives. They, or I should say the masses, don't even try to recall their dreams. But the dream state is there to protect all the data that goes through the mind, like a computer, and into the subconscious for later reference.

V: *So what I take from that is if we didn't dream to clear the path for the next day's journey, to perhaps, help sort out affairs, then we'd almost be like a robot?*

Dad: *Yes, in a way. If people say they don't dream, they are more than likely the ones that don't do much on a daily basis. No, I don't mean they don't work daily, but they don't stretch their imagination and step out of their comfort zone. Those that dream at night also and generally fervently dream while awake. In that, I mean, the great masters, the ones throughout human history who created mechanical devices or other gadgets to make the human existence more palatable paid attention to dream thoughts. Or, the ones that create new ideas and new venues that, in turn, help other creative minds take their thoughts a step further with each generation that proceeds. These creative minds may have gotten the `aha' moment within the dream state and paid attention to the information.*

V: Yes I know what you mean. Some in this life say they're bored and I can't for the life of me ever say I'm bored. It's just not possible from my viewpoint since there's so much to learn and do in my few years on the earth.

Dad: Exactly, you and I know how often I came up with various ideas to help save steps on a specific job or the one I recall perhaps in the late '90s was the idea of perpetual motion creating energy to one's home without using the utility companies' source of energy.

V: Yes, I remember, that was in 1998 when you came to my home. You drew out a plan that sounded very plausible and seemed as though it would work. But why didn't you go ahead with it?

Dad: Honey, you know I was in that church, which taught us that everything, was materialistic if one stepped out of the proverbial box and did something different. Thus all ideas I had were suffocated within that mindset.

V: I know. You also designed and created the shoulder strap for the automobile only to seal the envelope and never had it patented. I know you sent it to yourself. I wish I knew where that envelope was. Back then it was in the bureau drawer; however, you since purchased a newer set of furniture.

Dad: I kept it in my metal box for years. Your sister probably has it with all my papers.

V: *You also held back from a gift of a piece of prime property that you barbered at because of that religious belief, which could have turned you into a millionaire if sold. I don't fault you dad as that religious cult, kept me from having a full college education.*

Dad: *I am so pleased you all saw the hypocrisy and left. I too, left the religion for 8½ years only to jump back in after the World Trade centers were destroyed. Those old beliefs that Armageddon would come and kill all who didn't believe, honey, what a crock of bull! That religion was begun by a mere man that decided he didn't like the belief of another cult. That's all it was. How and why do so many cling to a religious belief when it began by a mere man? But of course, they all state it is directed by God.*

How can all religions be guided by God and simultaneously be different? It's beyond belief that I and millions followed and still follow aimlessly down a narrow path of belief. Plus, we turned away family members because they didn't believe as those of us blinded, no almost hypnotized by the leaders of such.

It's simply astonishing how the masters of those cult religious systems do that to humble followers.

Also, equally amazing is the fact that we didn't just feel the love from within ourselves, and realize spirituality has nothing to do with what a teacher told us. But to feel the love that exudes and comes with us via our spirits as we enter the earth's realm of the living.

V: *Wow, well stated. Yes, I'm pleased the four of us left that hypocritical line of thinking. You know Dad that religion never really drew me in. I mean it wasn't really in me. Oh, I liked the assemblies because I'd make new clothes and flirt with the guys. That was fun for me and knowing lots of people that are truly good; I liked that immensely. Knocking on doors and preaching about something that didn't sit well with me, I hated. I never wanted to go back to talk further like the cult taught over and over that we should do. Oh, I jotted down the little notes on the house to house record, but I rarely went back to visit anyone. I just played the game of go out on Saturday morning, Sundays before or after the cult meeting and Wednesdays too. I played the game of attending all the meetings. But you know I hated the fact that those Elders ruled over everyone and if you basically sneezed the wrong way you could just about get kicked out or their term disfellowshipped. Oh goodness, that was the worst of the worst because if disfellowshipped, you could no longer speak to any of your friends or family, nor they to you. And if disfellowshipped, you'd almost have a sizeable symbolic D posted on your forehead, noting rejection.*

Dad: *I always thought disfellowshipping a cruel punishment for being human. Yes, sleeping with another's mate is hurtful and wrong but why didn't the elders see that they are imperfect* too? *I always tried not to disfellowship ones in that circumstance but tried to counsel them to stop that line of action. Many thanked me years later for helping them through a tough time and not kicking them out.*

Honey, I didn't think I should do that because hey, I was just as human as they were. What right did I have to judge them that harshly?

V: *Really? I agree. We are all spiritual beings having a human experience. You know Dad I wonder….what it's like on other planets? I know we, on this one planet, can't possibly be the only planet that houses life forms. Are there others?*

Dad: *Oh, yes all over the many galaxies.*

V: *I wish I knew the names of others. Do you know the names?*

Dad: *There's **Optimus**, that has life forms that don't look like humans, but they have a beauty as well. Then there's **Spisterierious**, and they too have life forms. I don't know all the other names as of yet. I've been busy studying why I was placed on earth at that specific time.*

V: *What did you learn?*

Dad: *I learned that I specifically enlisted into that family. I also learned mom and dad didn't want to have any more children because mom was forty when she had me and was getting tired. But they did, and mom told me, I was a welcome surprise. I'm so glad I enlisted into that family. Honey they were and are so nice to me. But I enlisted to see what it was like to be a young boy with a respectful set of parents, plus to learn what humans go through in times of great distress like the depression. Also, to actually live through the various technical and mechanical items soon to be invented throughout my life. Indeed, it was a grand time to be born!*

I always liked Science as you know, but I didn't grasp it fully, however here I intend to learn all I can before I enlist again.

V: *So, you will enlist again?*

Dad: *Yes, I'd like to enlist when one of the grandchildren has a child. I won't enlist to be in that religious cult again, so I won't be enlisting if and when Debbie's children have children. That was a rough way of life, judging or being judged by mere humans. This next time, I want to be free of religion and have a metaphysical, spiritual happy existence in the Science field.*

V: *Oh, how grand! Maybe, if I'm still here, I'll be able to note that it's you. I want you to, let's see…..how about you, as a boy or girl, make the sound of a donkey, and you won't know why, but I will know it's my lovely father. Oh, that would be grand!*

Dad, it's been great as always. I'm sending a spiritual hug and tell all your family I've loved them for all my earthly existence, too.

Dad: *Tell the little ones I love them as well. And please tell Dwayne and my other children, I love them and all their babies too. I love Debbie's kids, but there's a difference in that they haven't seemed truly loving towards me. Oh, they put on airs, well the girls did, but the son was pretty balanced and seemed to come along okay. Till the next time and hey, don't make it so long!*

V: Okay, I'll make sure I contact you more often. Love you so very, very much, as do my babies and siblings.

Till then....

Dad: *By for now.*

Each time I channel my father, I can actually see him sitting on a bench with white flooring almost in a mist at his feet; the background is a beautiful sky blue.

Plus, there's a definite roof overhead help up with white pillars and a knowing, if you will, of serenity.

I feel and envisage that every time.

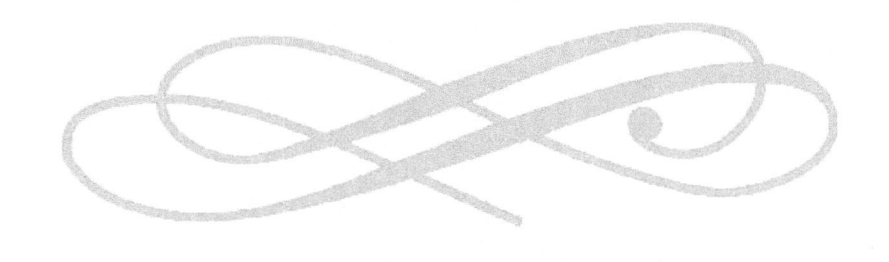

CHAPTER ELEVEN

Karma & the Bible

Today, July 25, 2013, 6:04 a.m. is a grand and beautiful sunny day of 82 degrees! Chatting with dad is a must!

V: *My sweet father, how are you?*

D: *I'm okay honey. How about you?*

V: *It's been a trying few months, but I made it through. I wonder, I know so little about Karma. Is there anything you could edify me about it, to share with others?*

Dad: *Karma is when one works out issues in life that may have disabled them on earth until they figure out what to do. Many feel if someone is doing terrible things, then karma will bring something dreadful to them, likewise if they do good, karma brings them good in return. For example, if a man kills another, which is despicable, he undoubtedly will bring ill will to himself. This person brings it upon himself and goes to prison if convicted. But what you really want to know is what happens on the other side right?*

V: *Right.*

Dad: *It's like this. When in physical life on earth, things happen for a reason. The reason is that when we return here, to the spirit realm, we're able to teach others of when they do something out of the ordinary, like kill someone, they will pay for it. Now some never get caught, but when they return to the other side where I am, they have learned many things to help others not to do what they did. Even though on earth it was cool to them that they didn't get caught.*

V: *Odd.*

Dad: *Yes, odd, however since they weren't captured before they came back here, they generally enlist to be birthed again into a mother and father that will teach them more lessons on earth. However, this next time they're sure to get caught, put in jail and or possibly killed for what they did.*

V: *Hmmm, is Karma a bad thing?*

Dad: *No, honey it isn't. Karma is just the means to an end. It's the beginning of what a spirit enlists for, to learn. To begin something there so they can learn a lesson, even though they are not conscious of why they are there. They have to go through the process to help others learn while here.*

V: *Seems like an essential aspect of living.*

Dad: *In a sense it is honey. It keeps spirits going back to the earthy realm to see what they might do next. Kind of like a story on earth when someone dreams and then writes about it afterward. This many times teaches earthly ones not to do what the other did within that story, or it shows them to follow along to do what happened before them. Thus a lesson learned, good or bad.*

V: *Amazing. Now, what have you and the family been up to of late?*

Dad: *Oh Bixby, it's been so enriching!*

V: *How so?*

Dad: *I've learned that your sister Debbie enlisted to earth to marry a controlling husband as she had and to determine what it was like to have cancer.*

V: *What, really? Spirits come here on purpose to experience diseases?*

Dad: *Yes, we do. She said she was under the impression people got it from smoking, but she never smoked. Therefore, she realized that cancer comes in various forms. Hers formed in her stomach, and because it was there, she knew it was from stress. Now, she knew that while on earth, but chose to keep silent about her husband causing her to acquire it. He was one of those silent but deadly people.*

You know honey I never knew he was like that, but you told me many times you felt he was a controlling, do-as-I-say person.

V: *Debby learned that too, but stayed with him anyway.*

Dad: *Yes, she did, but also to learn. Think of the things you'll be able to teach us when you arrive here. You'll be able to explain what it's been like to raise four children to adulthood without any male help. That's a task in itself, which I know from raising six children. Oh, by the way, she's felt bad that she allowed him to keep the two of you apart those last years.*

V: *Please tell her I understood the why, and don't hold her accountable. It was the way of the religion to do what the `master' husband instructed. Debby was a follower, not a leader; thus she did as instructed. Not me, I never ran with a pack. I made my own path, curvy it seems, to arrive at my goals, although I've made them just the same. I say curvy because when on this earth, we never know what obstacles will lead us this way or that, which makes the path curve.*

Dad *I'd like to know about your mother Fidella and grandfather, when did they meet and where? Where was that?*

Dad: *I'll let mom tell you.*

F: *Hi dear. You want to know when and where your grandfather and I met?*

V: *Yes, if you don't mind.*

F: *No, not at all. Midsummer, a yearly picnic was held at the fairgrounds. My parents and sisters and I were all excited about going there because when you live on a farm, you're pretty far away from many others. We had a large farm of two-*

hundred acres. Our father didn't let us girls drive into town without him, so the yearly town picnics were the thing to do. Your grandfather was so handsome. He loved to fight and when he'd walk into a group of men and if they'd say something the wrong way, why he'd haul off and hit them.

V: Really? When I knew him, he was, of course, older and seemed so calm. But then youth has its peculiarities.

F: Yes, it does. He had a scrap with one guy and walked away from the next one that threw a punch. He just happened to walk over to my side of the dance floor, saw me and forgot about the fight. The others seemed to let it go, too. He introduced himself and dusted off his britches, and I thought him handsome. We chatted a little bit and went to our respective homes. But he learned where I lived.

V: Was it in Vienna?

F: No, we lived outside of Vienna a few miles. We lived closer to Meta, MO. So to travel to the Fairgrounds in Vienna was half a day's ride. Anyway, he asked what town I lived in, and of course, I told him. Then one day about a month later he went into town, asking exactly where the Pendleton's lived. The lady at the general store told him where our farm was, and out he rode surprising us, actually me! He had a big piece of apple pie that momma gave him and a glass of fresh cow's milk. Boy, he loved that! He stayed about an hour and seemed shy when pa came home, so he left. But he said he'd visit again and did.

V: *How old were you?*

F: *I was sixteen. Soon he showed up again and a few months later we married.*

V: *Thank you grandmother, I wonder if there is anything in the newspapers about that picnic.*

F: *Should be, it seems they wrote about everything we did.*

V: *Is it out of the ordinary to have earthlings asks questions like this or do most, when you're summoned, ask about life after life?*

Dad: *Honey, it's like this. When I was on earth, I wanted to know everything there was about my family, my mother, my sisters, etc. And when I arrived here, it seemed that I already knew what was what without even asking a question. But if I were in your place and could call upon us, I'd do the same thing.*

V: *It's just so exhilarating life after life and the life before me. I loved the researching when I created your book dad. I just love to research and gain knowledge on almost any subject.*

F: *Dear, I wanted so much to learn all I could as a child and after becoming a wife and mother as well. I never stopped learning, as knowledge will bring you the greatest happiness while on earth. Each question you ask brings you closer to your answer. No question is foolish. So please come to us often, let us learn from you as you learn from us.*

V: *Oh, I intend to as often as I can. I do have another question about the religion we grew up in, Dad.*

Dad: *Yes, what is it?*

V: *Why do those in the religion* **think** *they are the only ones that know all about the Bible and is the Bible something that really came from God?*

Dad: *Now, that is an interesting question. I now believe that the Bible is a book that many wish to believe in. It's something that the masses long for, and the masses are mostly followers and need someone, something to cling to. Pastor Russell, as he called himself began his religion because he didn't like the current religious beliefs he was taught and decided to branch out on his own. Stating it was* **The Truth**, *but honey it was the truth as he perceived it. Just like so many other religions on earth that cause family separation, strife, and so many wars. Each believes their religious beliefs are the one and only.*

V: *Yes, but how can each religious belief encompass the only thought that is correct?*

Dad: *Exactly! All religions think their line of thought is correct and yet when I came here last year I was so wrong about that. Here, there is an automatic knowing that the thinking on earth is all manmade. Not one of those religions knows all there* is to know about the book called the Bible. The Bible, it's believed here, was made to create a stir within the world.

V: Why? Oh, I think I know. To teach various ways or thought patterns while here? And to see what transpires?

Dad: Yes, you got it! Without this Bible, which is mass produced and dissected by all religious beliefs, various thoughts may not have abounded. Do you see honey; this book has caused the masses to either be followers or leaders.

Followers in that many want something to believe in and carry on with their lives and others, the rare ones, want to be leaders; many in the name of the Bible.

But, the leaders are the ones that use the Bible perhaps to cause ones to follow them, maybe in a religious way or to follow them as a habit. Leaders utilize those of like mind to keep God or the energies that are, in their hearts and yet tread on them in other areas.

V: What do you mean? Like they use people to do what they want in the name of the Bible or God?

Dad: Yes, that's what I mean. When we're here after going through that situation, as I did, I realize I was used, under the guise of the religion, to do what those leaders wanted and you know I believed it hook line and sinker. But honey, I don't have any ill feelings and you shouldn't either because knowledge is what we learn through all the various aspects of life on earth.

V: *I do get it, and I see how leaders do that on a daily basis. Something else I've wondered about is why does this religion think they can kick people out when they've done a natural human thing like sex or just not choosing to believe in it anymore? I've always thought that very non-Christian. Or if alcoholism is wrong then why isn't obesity wrong as well?*

You know, many are disfellowshipped for having sex or alcoholism, but obese persons are never disfellowshipped for their obesity. All are obsessions if you will, but the major one singled out within the Jehovah Witness religion is sex. The others, to me, are worse than sex, by far.

Dad: *I see your point. Tragically, men have made the rules on earth and judged those that don't adhere to them. When someone returns home to where I am now and led a life of obesity or alcoholism or even sex out of wedlock, no one here looks down on them. Instead, we learn from their journeys. Do you remember when we first spoke, I told you we don't talk like you do, but we have a knowing that we almost automatically possess when we arrive?*

V: *Yes, I recall that.*

Dad: *When someone arrives within the parameters we're speaking of, we learn from the journey and then we know if we want to choose to enlist as that type of person when we return. Does that make sense?*

V: Yes, it does. I think it's amazing the knowledge that must exude from everyone you meet there.

Dad: Bixby, it's not overwhelming either. We grasp this knowing bit by bit. We, as on earth, take our time to learn. As we travel within this realm, we are touched by various ones that teach us silently, and yet effectively what we need to know and when we need to understand it.

Like when we decide to enlist into a particular being, mother or father, we're instantly and kindly flooded with specific knowing of this journey. This knowledge, in turn, allows one to take that journey or yet another.

On earth we know nothing of where we just came from and yet as children, we are the closest to our spiritual life.

Have you ever heard at various times, children have imaginary friends?

V: Sure.

Dad: These imaginary friends are spirits guiding the little ones to take their first steps as humans. Guiding them, if you will, and letting go. It's quite a process from this side. We see many new parents afraid of their child's actions and don't know what to do. Many take their little ones to doctors to find out what's wrong and yet there's nothing wrong. Parents merely nurture them until they are encapsulated by their parent's thoughts and can no longer see or hear us. It's a type of inner hearing that many experience when they reach their intuitive side.

V: *Interesting. I recall at the age of four-and-a-half, learning to read and write and I always wanted to have a pen and paper with me. Was I silently told I'd love to research and write?*

Dad: *It seems to be so.*

V: *I am fascinated with paper and pen; the texture and feel of the paper intrigues me. The way a particular pen smoothly glides along as I write. When I chose a journal to purchase, I always feel the pages first.*

Dad: *It's an exciting process, and you were meant to write.*

V: *Indeed! I'll have to prick your knowledge later. As always, love you!*

Dad: *Love you too. Call upon me soon, if you can.*

V: *I will. Bye, my love.*

CHAPTER TWELVE

De-ja-vu…Stars & Going Forward

This morning, November 1, 2014, I woke with a gnawing feeling to channel my father. I've been remiss for a while, no, actually inundated with estate sales, packing my own home and then moving into a condo, which indeed is not remiss….just extremely busy in the survival mode.

Now to continue, I've felt guilty not slowing down long enough to call upon my father for guidance and wisdom from beyond this earthly realm.

Thus, today, I'll ask my father a few more questions I've wondered about.

V: *Good morning dad or should I just say hello since you probably don't have time, morning, etc. wherever you are.*

Dad: *Hi honey. No, we don't have time here. We do pay attention and listen to spirits that came before us, receiving lessons that when we enlist to or return to earth, we will then have various knowledge when re-entering.*

V: *Like de-Ja-vu?*

Dad: *Yes, honey, like that. When I was on earth, there were times when I felt I knew this person or that person or felt I'd been in one place or another. Now, I know I had been wherever and did know those persons from a previous life.*

V: *It's interesting you brought that up because I've felt those same feelings and had those thoughts along life's highway too.*

I've done a great deal of genealogy over the past few years, as you know and in doing so, I became emotionally close to past relatives. Within that research, I found a relative of your fiancé' Theresa Tillman, and it turns out she was looking for her grandfather. You may or may not have known this at the time or over the many years while you remained on the earth, but you and Theresa Tillman had a son, which is now wherever you and Theresa are. Have you met him? Has Theresa told you of him?

Dad: *Oh, yes, I've met him.*

V: *What's he like? I've met two of his three daughters, Pat and Tina, the other sister, died several years ago. Perhaps you've met her also.*

Dad: *Yes, I've met them all. As you know one of the previous times you contacted me, I was talking to Theresa. I learned that after we split, she lived her life deceitfully in that she had a few men in her life, and a husband that was abusive. She told me if* we had stayed together she didn't know if she would have been good for me or not. Because she was so miserable with all the other men, she killed herself in 1979 over her heartache of not being with me.

V: Really? Well, that's awful. Our mother, we know, was never a passionate lover towards you nor did she hold the love I think you missed by not marrying Theresa Tillman. However, if you had married Theresa, you would never have had me or my siblings. I'm pleased as punch you married our mother!

Dad: Yes, honey, it was a sorrowful parting. I loved her so much as I told you when there. She was a heart breaker to be sure. But I couldn't and wouldn't marry into a family where the father had been an accomplice to a murder and went to prison. I met her after he got out of prison. He drank so much, slurring his words all the time because he ran a moonshine business, which bothered me. You know I never got drunk after a bit in the Navy. I always wanted to know what I was doing at all times.

V: You must have said that to us growing up because I've never been drunk either. I, too always want to know what I'm doing, therefore no drugs or over drinking on my part either. It's a shame that you and Theresa loved each other so much and couldn't go forward with it, but I know how that is. I woke with a dream of a man I loved in my teens, and we too parted. I've carried a special kindness for him all these years. In the dream this morn he told me he has loved me always and asked me to marry him. We married that very day since time is of the essence on earth.

Dad: *Please tell my newly found granddaughters, I said hello and that I'm sorry I never knew Theresa had a son. Had I known, you know I would have done the right thing and married Theresa. But she never contacted me. I haven't asked her, but maybe she followed me where I worked and found out I married and had children. She died young waiting for me here. She never enlisted again, just waited for me. It's kind of nice to know that honey, someone, loved me so much that she waited for me. However, here there's no time. Things seem to come and go in flashes of energy. There's no accounting of seconds, minutes, hours, and we certainly know about the science of things. Oh, you know how much I love science!*

V: *I sure do. You always spoke of the speed of light and how the earth turns on its axis precisely in time for each season etc.*

Dad: *Now I realize it is so. It is precisely made so that earth and each planet out there, yes there are other planets we can enlist to. I'm thinking about **Hermese**. I want to enlist there to see what it's like.*

V: *I wonder if other planet inhabitants look different than us or are they all human beings that look like us. Of course, if TV hadn't been invented, I wouldn't ask that question, and because of the many movies and TV shows that portray life on other planets as monster-like ones, I wonder what they look like.*

Dad: *TV was nice, but you know I didn't watch much. I liked to read and discern other things. Recently I comprehended another way to learn besides mental transference of thought. Here we gain knowledge by going to a type of table, and peer into it to see what we wish to know and then choose that subject matter. Recently, I peered into it and noted something unheard of on earth.*

V: *What was that?*

Dad: *Of course there's an endless supply of things unknown to earthlings as well as other planet dwellers. But this was about the stars. The stars are made similar to the earth and yet very different. They have what you could relate to as light. However, the light we saw and you observe in the skies at night is merely a type of phosphorus mineral. Its name is very different from phosphorous, but you understand that name. The name is actually Erkin.*

V: *Erkin, is that the correct spelling?*

Dad: *I think it's Erkiin, with two i's, but I've never been a great speller.* He chuckled!

V: *Okay, interesting. I'll research to locate anything about Erkiin or Erkin. What else about the stars?*

Oh my goodness! I found this informational link! *"Potentially mobile phosphorus in Lake Erken sediment!"*
[ii]*https://www.sciencedirect.com/science/article/abs/pii/S0043135499003759*

Elemental phosphorus was first isolated (as white phosphorus) in 1669 and emitted a faint glow when exposed to <u>oxygen</u>" meaning "light-bearer" (Latin *<u>Lucifer</u>*), referring to the "<u>Morning Star</u>", the planet <u>Venus</u>." https://en.wikipedia.org/wiki/Phosphorus

Dad: *They do eventually burn out and fall from the galaxies as we believed on earth. But the reason they fall and burn out is as they burn, the exterior of each star disintegrates to a small level which takes away their capability of staying in the galaxy. Thus, they fall at that time.*

V: *Hmmm, that **is** interesting. I bet if I told someone that here, they'd think I was nuts. But you know dad when people on earth think out of the proverbial box, most think them nuts anyway. So, I'll gladly remain in a diverse category. I love to think out of the box, which is a gift you gave me and all your children. We may have grown up in a particular religion, with strict rules of how a man thought it should be, which the principles were and are good. However, it stunted our mental growth for twenty to thirty years or more until we figured out that there was and is so much more to learn while here.*

Dad: *It's true, so true. Humankind has a way of following those that think out of the box, as you say, and then wondering why all others don't think like them. Well, I'll tell you why. All that enlist to the earthly realm enlist to learn from the parents they chose to come from and those parents wanted to enlist through their parents and so on. That way all are learning at different speeds and different preferences. Hence different religions, schools, styles, etc. etc. The list is endless on earth.*

V: That makes total sense! I was told by one of my sisters when I was in my twenties, that I was a risk taker. At first, it hurt my feelings because I do run on my own to make things work out. But in hindsight, she saw me as one that thinks out of the box. Yes, I'm alone because men have told me I intimidate them and they think I don't need them, which is untrue. I'd love to have a partner, but I do insist, not verbally, but inwardly that I won't take another man on, unless he is a quality person, one of intelligence and sincerity. I know all things are possible with prayer and conviction, but I'm not ready for that scenario.

I do love you, dad. Always have, always will. I'm not afraid to be here. I think it's because I've stayed away from the harsher elements during this life and hopefully have taught my children to do the same.

I'll continue to call upon you and the other relatives, in the beyond, to help us at various times as I have since you've moved on.

To me, of course, all my babies are brilliant, how could they not be by having such a wonderful grandfather, a guide for the father they never had and a pretty good earthly mother too. I know they would say that and have. They've stated of their friends' parents never accomplishing much and how I keep trying to do more. It's made me who I am, to go forward even though adversity has struck me down many times.

Dad: Honey, that's what makes a great human, adversity! Yes, it hurts when it strikes, but those like you that go forward and try something new, in turn, helps others see that if she or he can go ahead then certainly I can go forward within my trials and tribulations. Yes, I have always believed that going forward through times of trouble on earth, made me a better man, a better person, who could then help others. It's not always about giving money to others, yes that helps on earth, but it's the giving of one's self that helps others. They see charitable gifts and realize at a point in their life that if they pay their knowledge forward, then, they too succeed.

V: I get it. I've told my four children that **IF** they try, they never fail. But **IF** they never try, that's when they fail in this life.

Dad: Honey, you've meant a lot like me. In that, you keep going. You kept and still keep figuring out what to do next to proceed in a manner of fact, toward any goal you wish. It has taken you far. I want you to encourage others to step out on that limb of doubt and jump off it, as you've done consistently while there. That in itself enables others to take the leap and see what lies beyond doubt.

V: *Yes, I certainly take leaps of faith. Doubt, is but a feeling, a word. It can cause one to freeze in their tracks or jump beyond the fear of uncertainty. I love taking chances to see what I can do with each wish I put out there. Of course, I know that when I do that, something opens up for my passage into what I previously somewhat feared, and yet passed through yet another door. I love it!*

Dad: *Please continue to do so. Your life on earth is a healthy one and should be enjoyed. I will happily help with your prayers and your children. They need help, and all of us here have been through various trials, doubts, and fears. Hence we can help and always do any time we are requested.*

V: *So we must request what we want, like in prayer?*

Dad: *Yes, on earth it's called prayers, and here it's just within our thoughts. You all do it down there, or at least most do. Just a simple prayer spoken within the mind causes those of us that have gone before, to help in any way we can.*

Now, I want you to note, that some who have enlisted on earth, have enlisted to learn various conditions and problems. We can lead them as far as they have enlisted to be directed to. Does that make sense?

V: *Yes, I get it. If an enlisted one only wants to go so far, then that's all he or she wants to learn. Very sad for the family left behind, but yes, I do get it.*

Dad, I'm going to have to leave yet again. These sessions exhaust me and yet they thrill me to have you still in my life. Oh, I'd love to hear your laugh and see your real smile again; however, I know you stayed as long as you enlisted for.

Before I go, do you know when I think of you, I get misty through the days and now years?

Dad: *I feel things here that I didn't there. No, I don't see you each time you cry or are sad over me, but I feel a sense of something somber at times.*

V: *It's probably one of your babies missing their wonderful father.*

Love you always, and I will speak to you again. Soon I trust.

I have to add, the information about the stars and galaxies is something I've never read nor heard of, although, previously I, in no way thought to research the science of the stars. Thus, I know for a fact I'm not making any of this up!

CHAPTER THIRTEEN

Family-Past Lives & Patrick Henry

A snowy, icy day is upon us this Sunday, February 15, 2015. I love these kinds of days. It's a bit overcast too, hence a cup of tea and a chat with my father is in order. What could be better?

V: *Good morning my lovely father.*

Dad: *Hi honey. How are you?*

V: *I'm doing ok. I've moved to a smaller location with fewer bills and a swimming pool to boot!*

Dad: *Oh, you love to swim. We used to go as a family to several pools, creeks, and camping. You swam so well.*

V: *Yes, I loved it then and will be tickled to swim this summer. Dad, I have more questions. Ok?*

Dad: *Sure what do you want to know this time?*

V: *This may sound silly, but I've wondered about Aunt Tessie. Is it possible for her to tell me where that Charleston contest was that she won? Also, Dwayne and I have so often driven to*

Vienna and Iberia, MO to find the location of what you stated was Margaret Jarrett's gravesite. However, we found it several years ago when I wrote your life history in the Ankle Express book, that she is buried in the Jarret Cemetery, in Fairview, which is not the location you previously drove us to.

So do you know the exact location of the gravesite you drove Dwayne and I separately and our families to? It's down a two-lane blacktop highway on the right side (of course depending on which way you're traveling) there was an open meadow between two small hills on either side. The gravesite is on the left hillside with perhaps fifteen to twenty stones midway up the slope in amongst many trees. Do you recall?

Dad: *Yes, it's on hi-way C.*

V: *Where's hi-way C?*

Dad: *Honey it might be called a number as well. But it's close to Jeff City. See if you can find that highway. But it's not Margaret Jarrett's site it's one of my aunts or uncles. I think Johnny Gray for some reason.*

V: *Can you tell me if it's still there or has someone removed it?*

Dad: *No, it's still there.*

V: *Hmm, I'll see if I can locate it. Thanks for the information.*

Now, Aunt Tessie, is she there?

Dad: *Yes, she heard you.*

Tessie: *Hi sweetie. How have you been? I've noted you've had many struggles through your life, but somehow you managed it all pretty well.*

V: *Yes, there's been a host of struggles; however, I've learned to think differently, and I have an inner knowing that all will be okay, no matter what. I've taught my children to know this as well. When I have little money, I know that the Universal energies are never late. I know that even though my pocketbook looks bare, it's just **a matter of letting go of the thought of less to receive more; it always arrives just in time**.*

Tessie: *Yes, that's extraordinary energy you carry. When Ross and I had our struggles, we carried something similar with us. We knew that together we could tackle anything and come out on top. As you know, we had no children and as adults on earth that's the one thing most people want. However, without children, we were able to acquire wealth. We bought the land near Jeff City in Holt Summit, built a store and a home.*

V: *Yes, I loved that house.*

Tessie: *It was a good one. But the thing dear is that we kept going forward. Many on earth seem to get all tensed up when things move away from what they want. They forget that they are taken care of just like animals. A bird is taken care of when he or she flies about finding food in various places. No, they don't plot out how to get the food, they just go about their* business, and there it is. Funny, how the energies on earth take each of us down various paths. But Vickie, the **one thing the masses don't do, is that they never move out of their own way!**

They tend to think they have to have this or that burden and I might say it's good they do because when they return here, they have many lessons to teach us. These lessons prompt us to reenlist as your father told you, to have more knowledge of what type of family they want to be born into. I wanted a father who was kind since in the previous life my father was a brute to my mother and me. I was an only child, which made me not want children in the next life. Thus I met and married a man that couldn't father a child nor was I to be a mother. We wanted children while on earth because that's what all married couples or most want. However, we didn't know we'd requested that type of life before arriving on earth's scene.

V: *Funny you should say that. When I was sixteen, I wanted to get married, but when I reached eighteen, I realized I didn't want to marry. However almost two years later I did marry. During those teen years, I thought I didn't want any children because I wanted all my things to be in order, at all cost. However, a higher source knew better, which I'll probably notice it was my requirements when I enlisted in this life. I have four wonderful adult children. Oh, I've had my encounters with various happenings, if you will, while raising them and even since they're grown. But these many learning experiences are shaping me, to help others when I return home, which I now know and perhaps help others here.*

Tessie: *Yes, you understand. Now the Charleston contest you wondered about and Victor couldn't recall because he was only four or five when Una and I went to Westphalia and then to St. Louis. St Louis is where the main contest took place and Westphalia is where we were chosen to travel to the competition. I was so angry because the newspaper stated Una won the contest and I was the second runner up. However, it was the opposite. I won the contest, and she was the second runner up. I was so mad but soon got over it because we knew the difference. What fun we had!*

Victor, did you ever teach your kids how to dance the Charleston? Remember we showed you often.

Dad: *Yes, Tessie I taught them the Charleston, frequently. That was about the only dance I knew when the kids were little. Do you remember Bixby?*

V: *Yes, I do. I've shown my kids many times when they were growing up too.*

I have a question, and I think you answered it before, but I'd have to reread parts of this information to know. It's about Theresa Tillman.

Dad: *You asked if I knew I had a son with her. Yes honey, I now know and our son is here too. Terence.*

V: *Well, how can I prove it to those living here? I've met Theresa's granddaughters Patty and Tina, but I need more proof before I can tell all my siblings, however, Dwayne knows and has met them. But I believe the other three may not think it's true even though I knew it was true the moment I read a notice online from Patty. Are there any others now living that would know of this? Or where can I find another connection?*

Dad: *No, I don't think anyone is alive that would know. But, we were engaged for several months, and we did get together several times. You now that Nash car I had to let go of?*

V: *Yes.*

Dad: *Well, that was the car we dated in, and I told you that was a heart breaker when I let her go.*

V: *I thought that might be. But now you're with her and your son. I still need to find a bit more proof before I say anything about this. We did a DNA test, which only proves we were all from European descendants but can't find actual connections online to establish this connection, logically to my siblings.*

To change the subject what else have you learned there dad?

Dad: *Honey, I've learned as much as you might have guessed. One thing I've learned over these two-plus years is that all the enlisted ones come back with the knowledge of where they were in time and information of their current parents.*

V: *Hmm interesting. I've done a few past life regressions and learned in one that I was Patrick Henry's wife. I saw him orate on a porch, between white pillars and a red brick building.. Because women weren't allowed, I dressed like a man and sat on a buckboard, to see my Patrick. I will have to go back to my journal and place that wonderful information in this book or another book on that subject. Simply amazing the things I saw and drew and the time period was spot on!*

I've come to believe in past lives. Why not? My past religion disabled all of us from knowing or better yet from even thinking of anything of that sort.

It's been a fantastic journey and when I had the dream of Henry Ford; I saw a past life then, which caused me to write my first book. Plus after researching about Henry Ford, I learned that the information I received was, in fact, correct. But my point is this, because of that dream I began to read books on top of books about dreams and metaphysics. Thus, I soon learned that what one receives in a dream or a past life experience is more than likely a real-life experience. Guess I shared that with the masses where you are too, before I came back again!

Dad: *Honey those living now and those from the past lend a hand to enlighten earthly ones seeking more knowledge outside of their religious barriers. They are the ones that help others open up to life beyond the norm of day to day human life.*

I love the fact that many of the enlightened ones aren't afraid to share their knowledge with ones that literally need to know this information.

These, in turn, help others become open-minded to a higher level of consciousness. It's incredible that now those who are informed have the freedom to share unlike the witches of Salem. They were enlightened and needed to share and yet killed. All those in the surrounding areas and most in the United States believed those that held higher knowledge were in fact witches. Interestingly, the clergy were and are held in such high esteem during that time as now, had a hand with the witch trials carrying on. They also knew various spiritual things; however they were never labeled as witches nor condemned to death.

V: An interesting thought, to be sure. I'm so pleased to share this information freely from you and our relatives. Plus, I won't be looked down upon or thrown in jail because I know what I know to be true.

If only the masses of men would stop these terrible wars. It's beyond me that they seem to believe fighting will make or turn others into what they deem is their truth. Just like Hitler and many other mass destroyers of humanity. How foolish when one is forced to believe one way or another out of fear. I'm sure during Hitler's time all those Jews that eventually lost their precious lives to Hitler's disgusting torturous orders must have thought many ways to kill that beast and all his subjects. But then they would have been just like him.

How horrible that he came here to destroy so many and yet he wanted all to be Arians, blue-eyed, blond hair. So, one might ask, where did he fit in? He was a complete opposite with black hair and dark eyes. Amazing isn't it?

Dad: Yes, and I've met him and some of the other mass murderers here.

V: Really? Do tell.

Dad: Now that they're here they can't believe all they did to destroy and conquer. Hitler himself has stated through thought transference that even though the masses hated him, he had to do what he had to do. It was as if an inner force pushed him to do it.

V: Goodness, I think he was just plain crazy! And yet all you've taught me thus far proves that he must have enlisted to become that kind of a mass killer to share the awful stories when he returned home. There's no excuse for mass killing. I'm still a human who doesn't understand that.

Dad: Maybe he was. But he chose to experience that life on earth. Such a horrible life it was, all the killing and so much unnecessary heartbreak. He has stated he never wants to enlist into that type of life form ever again.

V: I'm so pleased we were born after that time. We have evil bastards still here and not just in foreign countries. There are evil ones nearby and in all large cities as well. Foreign *countries seem to have it the worst though, in that they have people just like Hitler springing up all over the place. So much mass destruction abounds over there.*

It's shameful how humans react to their circumstances. Why don't they realize living in harmony is so much easier? I just don't get it.

Dad: *Honey, if everyone lived in peace and harmony, there'd be little to contrast the good and no one would know right from evil.*

V: *True, but all this suffering is a shame. Dwayne and I have discussed often the why's of all this strife.*

Like why are we placed on a planet of sickness and death of babies? If there is a God, then why do we have all the diseases, killings and death?

What does it prove?

Is there really a spirit being called God? Or is that entity merely named by humans via a book called the Bible? And if there is a God, then why does he or she allow all this suffering? Are we the puppets? Are we here to entertain this being?

Dad: *Interesting questions. First, there's not,* **a God**, *energy like people believe on earth. There is, however, a specific energy that created all the planets and all the vegetation, etc. on each planet.*

Each planet's inhabitants think differently than those on earth. Each knows there's an energy that created their life form and their type of vegetation.

As for children's deaths from diseases, that is what these children enlisted to learn. Some of the children's diseases cause others to invent something that helps many others.

V: *I have thought that before. There again is the contrast to bounce off of, but there's immense sadness within their precious parents. Yes, I know its lessons to share in the spirit realm, and yes, I'm human here. It's just so terribly depressing.*

Dad: *And then all these Hitler type beings create a type of energy in others, of what to do and how to do it, to stop this adversity. Do you understand? If these horrible ones didn't birth to this life, then many changes that need to take place may never have happened.*

V: *I understand, but it's so brutal. Mothers never want to send their babies overseas to fight other countries wars. We want our babies safe. I think if women were in control and not men, there certainly would be more peace.*

Dad: *I often thought that too. However, when we enlist, we are birthed to cause change on the earth. The energy called God is just a name those that have no real goals on the planet have something or someone to believe in. It's just that simple, honey. Many are born into families that go from one way of living to the next via the next generation. These are the people that fill in* the gaps of the working class. Those that invent and think outside the proverbial box are the ones that change the masses or enlighten them to other ways of thought. Does that make sense?

V: Yes, I believe it does.

Dad, I'm exhilarated and yet exhausted again. I'll have to stop for now. I wish it didn't fatigue me so much, as I love talking to my precious father.

Oh, one more thing. Have you visited telepathically with our mother?

Dad: Yes, but not often. It seems she served her purpose and just moved past me. But I know in her strange way she loved the children she bore while on earth.

V: Really? She had a funny way of showing it, very cold and unloving.

Dad: Yes, she was like that but again, it's because of her upbringing with a drunkard father and a kind mother. Regretfully, she took after the father and sorry for the way she treated all the kids. Call upon me again my little Bixby.

Love you all so very much!

V: Love you too so very much.

Till the next time.

While rewriting this book, I located this **Pre-Birth** session, in one of my early journals from **November 15, 2001.** Today is Monday, December 21, 2018, 9:44 a.m. I did several pre-birth and past life regressions during this time, utilizing tapes by Dick Sutphen.

I wrote: I went from my body lying on my bed to an altered state above my house, five-hundred feet above, as instructed. I saw a large brick courthouse with huge pillars and wide front steps from a view off the street looking up. The sun shone radiantly behind it, early morning.

I then came to my parents to learn kindness, and saw a helmet and breast shield from Viking times. It was mine, I had been a warrior, but this time I came not to fight but to learn kindness and help others help themselves. I also, saw my three guides in long gold robes. The eldest hugging me as he pulled me to his chest, as though to say, you are well, all is well. I pulled away, his hands now on my shoulders, to smile. He smiled and nodded back.

The one next to him attired the same and the other also, smiling, handing me a large bag of money, an endless supply in a gold wrap without speaking. They told me the supply is endless and is coming very soon, to accomplish all I desire. It abruptly ended there.

I quickly sketched what I saw as I wrote this past life. I believe our thoughts indeed *gift* us what is intended at the very moment it's needed.

I feel and felt when I recently went through my journals, that this, for some reason, wanted me to place it within these pages. This information may allow others to step out of their comfort zone, and into their higher level of consciousness to possibly have a pre-birth or a past life regression session.

As you'll note within these pages, I came from a strict religious foundation, which forbade gaining knowledge *from the other side.*

When I received the very vivid dream of Henry Ford, November of 1995, that turned out to be factual of him, I knew I had to research the meaning. The knowledge I gained moved me to chat with dad and share my precious father's thoughts from the other side. Something I never imagined possible before the dream and research that ensued.

CHAPTER FOURTEEN

Skeptism

Throughout these chats from the other side, I've seriously thought I must be nuts! How can this happen and yet it's certainly not my imagination. I can't recall anything except that I chatted with my father or one of the relatives. When I reread it, I'm pleased with the connection and the information that came through.

My eldest brother, Dwayne, gifted me a book someone gifted him during the summer of 2016, stating that he found it interesting and I might also. Goodness! When I saw the title, The Afterlife of Billy Fingers, I couldn't wait to read it! It took a few short hours to read. Because the author went through various feelings, chats and sightings as I have, I instantly connected with her story, which confirms my truth too.

Shortly after receiving that book, my younger brother, called me on his way to work with a question that I don't recall. However, the conversation went from a simple good morning, how are you, to me telling him that I chat with dad via meditation.

In his skeptical way, he said, "Now why should you be able to talk to dad and not me?" His tone was almost angry.

"Well, let me read some of the beginning, and maybe you'll see how amazing it is".

He said, "Okay."

I read as he drove half an hour towards his construction job. Once he told me he arrived, I said, "I better let you go into work."

"No, I want to hear more, this is amazing! Do you actually think this is from dad? How can that be?"

I explained carefully and kindly of what I've read on the subject. I then said, "I've educated myself by reading many metaphysical books on the subject of dreams and meditation that state it's always the one that pays attention to what others pass off as nonsense, and that they are the ones that receive the information. However, not only do I pay attention, I believe it is possible. If you begin to learn more about meditation and metaphysics, I'm sure you'll start to open to the possibility of this as a reality.

Not only is this as it is, Dwayne, gifted me a book, which is a dynamite story of a woman's brother, coming to her after he passed. The similarities are amazing! At first, this calling upon dad was a way of healing for me, which I never realized would turn into a book. I just wanted to chat with dad."

He said, "This is so interesting; would you read a little more, please?"

So I read to page seventeen and said, "I don't want to keep you from your job."

"I wish I could hear all of it, but I do need to get to work. That's just amazing! Thanks for reading it to me."

"You're welcome; I'll give you a copy when it's finished, if it ever is."

"Ok."

Off to work he went and I continued to peruse this information. I'm still amazed at what comes forth.

There are all types of skeptics that show up in a person's life, no doubt about it. However, it's what we do within the Skeptism that makes a difference in our lives.

Listen to learn...
Meditate to relax...
Open to something more...
Research all that eludes you...
Step out of the proverbial box...
Live an enlightened life!

CHAPTER FIFTEEN

Gnats...Butterflies & Seeing Energies

For several hours last week and this morn, September 16th, 2018, I took time to help an aspiring new author with the formatting of her book. It's about her son who passed, and he too visits her and her family via gnats and butterflies.

In an email, I reiterated my story of dad to her about gnats kissing and or helping me, plus I sent the cup of tea picture that read hi, in chapter six.

Below, is part of what I wrote to her explaining yet another form, a seeing, of a loved one coming through to me as well.

...

Good morning:

When I woke this morn, I had a compelling feeling to finish formatting your book. I've taken time because I have great admiration and love to and for you and the memory of Bobby. (It turned out the next day; she emailed me of her niece wanting to finish the final editing of her book over the next few days and did. Now I realize why my guides and angels pushed me to finish formatting that very day and not put it off.)

I think I've mentioned to you earlier that when I'm working on my father's book, Life after Life, he's all around it too, in the form of a gnat. He's also around me when I drive. I also, think he's protecting me at various other moments in time. It's such an astonishing process.

Also, as I formatted your book, not only did I have one gnat, but I had two! I knew my father was there prodding me on and yet the other gnat was full of vim and vigor! (I knew it was her son Bobby, pushing me, annoying me to get it done now!) After maybe two hours of two gnats continually lying on, flitting and running around my hands as I typed, I had enough. I told them I loved them both, but I had to have my peace to continue. One automatically left. It really did, and I knew it was Dad. But the other one persisted. I swatted at it, and it stayed away. I must note, gnats generally fly around plants or foods, and I have neither on the second floor nor did I have any old food lying about my desk and there's only one live plant in my entire home.

Plus, I want to share what happened last week while in Murray, KY, where my grandson Edmond and I stayed.

I love researching family ancestry, which this time was in the nearby town of Paris, TN, where my mother grew up, when another spiritual event happened.

When we first arrived, Helian, the lady owner of Murray Lodge told me that her dear husband had died this past March; he was eighty-six and she forty-five. She'd read about me and my Estate Sale Made Easy book after I made the online reservation, and stated she'd order it after our chat and did. The fact that she was interested in my book brought on a more extended conversation of how I see, hear and feel those that have passed. Thus, when I walked in to leave the key a few days later, she asked me if I heard from her husband. She even asked if I saw anything else because she prayed that morning asking if he was there, stating she couldn't tell.

I knew what I received would help her immensely, so Edmond and I stayed to chat. We sat and talked about what I received of her husband the day I arrived, which was on Sunday and each of the three days thereafter.

I never saw a picture of him nor knew his name till our chat Wednesday.

At any rate, after I brought my items into my home for the next few days, I told her I kept seeing him smiling; while he looked upon the vast array of flowers all around the U-shaped motor lodge. I added I saw him on the roof at the center of the main building and asked if he repaired the roof while here. She said, "No, he never fixed the roof, but he did a great deal of research for the perfect roof in 2003, when he bought the motel and later the new roof."

I knew there had to be more to the *roof story*. As we chatted, she inquired, "Did you see what my husband wore?"

That may have been a strange question to some; however, it made perfect sense to me. I told Helian, I kept seeing her husband with white hair, thin and wearing a khaki zippered windbreaker jacket.

Immediately, she stood without speaking, walked into her home just beyond the check-in counter and brought back a khaki zippered jacket and said with tears streaming down her cheeks, "Is this what you saw? He wore this every single day, even when it became dirty."

"Yes, that's what I saw him in." She was amazed and clutched the jacket ever so tightly. I went on to acquaint her with the idea of those that pass arrive here in different forms, thus telling her of my gnat story. Sweetly, she asked if she shouldn't kill or swat away the gnats. I said, "I thank my father for coming to me each time, but if he's so persistent to linger on my hands or face, I do swat and sometimes kill it, knowing the gnat is merely a representation of my father allowing me to note he's with me. He's not living in the gnat." She was relieved, stating she will pay better attention.

··········

The email continued...Thus, when I'm helping another understand this fantastic concept of Life after Life in the form of gnats and in your case, also black butterflies, it helps when I tell my own story.

To continue the story, I told Helian that without a doubt her husband is there. I felt it all over the plants! Then she said, "He must be here because he planted all the plants and loved them!" She was extremely grateful stating she'd call his daughter to tell her what I saw of her father.

We said our farewells, and went back to our room to grab the suitcases to finish packing the car.

While Edmond and I were in the car, just about to leave, I saw Helian quickly walk behind my car and tap on my window to exclaim, "Victoria, Victoria....I'd forgotten, we had a terrible storm about a month ago, and the back side of the right arm of the u-shaped building was hit during that storm, and the shingles blew off! My husband was telling you about the roof, and now I must fix it! Thank you so much for telling me he is here! I will pay attention from now on."

I then got out of the car, turned slightly to my right to view the roof I saw her husband on and asked, "I have to ask more of your husband and the roof. Are you sure he never worked on the roof?"

"No, he never worked on the roof. However, the day before he died, he was up on that light post changing the light bulb. The light had to be changed by him lifting the top half of the post (about 8') off the lower part, take it down, change the light bulb, and then back up the ladder to lift that 8' poll up and back onto the lower post. It was very heavy and caused him to have a heart attack, which he died soon after."

"Ah, I now understand what I saw."

From the angle of my room, my vision showed her husband on the roof, when in fact; he'd been on the light post. See the picture on the following page, of the actual light post in reference to the tallest center roof.

The black post, in the background, is the one he climbed up on. If you look closely you'll note from the left side - room 19, it seemed as if he was on the roof and yet, he was on the post in front of the 2nd story roof, seen right-appearing `as if' on that roof.

Paying attention, is the key to connections on the other side.

CHAPTER SIXTEEN

Listen is the key

Upon waking this Wednesday morning, February 13, 2019, as usual, I grabbed my journal and jotted down, I need to chat with dad about prayer and wondered when I should stop this edition. Both my thoughts were answered within this very session!

V: *Good morning dad. I've spoken to you in between writing as always. But I felt the need to talk to you today about prayer and the importance of it. Ok?*

Dad: *Sure honey, hi. What's your question?*

V: *First how have things been there?*

Dad: *Oh, honey it's been such a miraculous way of learning spirituality. I've learned all that enlist become whatever they enlisted into. In that, we choose to become a new earthly life based on what the parents are doing at any given time, as I've stated. Parents are selected by who they are, where they live, and what time frame they live in. What type of people they are etc. It's been an altering experience to be a part of this* understanding. Soon I will come through to the earthly life again. You will know who I am.

V: *Really? I keep thinking you'll come back via Ashley's new baby. We shall see. If I note Victor mannerisms, I'll know, to be sure.*

I want to hear more, but for now prayer.

Dad: *Sure honey, shoot.*

V: *So I woke thinking of prayer and how vastly important it is to me. I pray to you often, and I know you answer my prayers usually in minutes! Yes, I know you've heard my pleas.*

Dad: *Honey I do hear all my babies prayers and their babies prayers too. I make sure when asked to include my family and all work to fulfill these desires. I know when you throw your hands up to the Universe and you actually tell the Universe, spirits guides, me and family to do your thing to make estate sales comes to life or whatever. We hear you.*

V: *Yes, I do that, and sometimes I've felt foolish throwing my hands up open wide to encompass all that hear me. Then I ask for what I intend to happen and close with my hands over my heart and say, it is so. I've done this since I learned about metaphysics from the School of Metaphysics.*

Dad: *You went to a school to learn that?*

V: *Yes, I had that dream of Henry Ford and Victoria Zane, remember?*

Dad: *I do honey, that was a fantastic dream. You know don't you that Victoria Zane and Henry Ford came to you to help you write that first book.*

V: *Yes, I've since learned that when a person is ready for information, it is given and in that case, a vortex opened on the last Friday of three weeks of dreadful migraines. I knew upon waking that day, November 1993 that the information gifted me, needed written down.*

Dad: *But honey now that I'm here having this awesome, magical, spiritual experience I know that it was no accident. They came to you because you needed to know that spiritual life is a reality, a reality that most humans fail to pick up on, as I mentioned earlier in our chats.*

V: *So my leaving the church after thirty-six years and never praying for years because I was angry, which somehow helped me. Hmmm, then migraines came to me, opening a vortex of knowledge and in turn a nudging from within, to write a book. This dream caused me to learn more from the School of metaphysics etc. etc., is that what you mean?*

Dad: *Honey, not praying was your way of leaving that religious way of belief behind. You connected prayer to that former way of life. It may have taken years to turn you around, but you got it! Most never pay attention to what is genuinely moving them along their natural path.*

V: *I see...yes, it took perhaps 10-years for me to realize prayer wasn't just within the religion of Jehovah's Witnesses, but it is something that all can do to connect to their spirituality beyond this earth. I get it and got it!*

Dad: *Isn't it miraculous? The fact that you paid attention to what mattered, is extraordinary. And that you've taught your children to go forward with open minds. I wish I hadn't been a part of that religious experience because I now know that religion is at the heart of most wars and separates many from those they love on earth.*

V: *It's undoubtedly a huge dividing point. I wish I could help many turn their lives around and search within, instead of what they see within their conscious realm of experience. When we, on earth, move past the mere conscious reality and seek from within, all aspects of earthly life make sense. It becomes, to me and for me, a path to my spiritual existence from whence I and all derive from. I love how things have transpired in my earthly life. From never wanting children to having four, the most of all my siblings and you know I've learned of numerology too, just a bit. I know that the number four means Angels of which I note daily. Often numbers line up in all fours, so I know without a doubt that my Angels, you and my spiritual guides are with me. I now pray often dad, so very often. I pray for knowledge and help with my son Blake. I pray for his help. I pray directly to you, dad, your parents, and siblings for you to send a shock or something from within him to change his ways of addiction. Oh, dad, I can't believe I asked to learn this lesson, but I know I must have asked for it because it's hitting me straight on!*

Dad: *Yes, honey you asked for it. Its part of what we do here when we want to become birthed again. The lessons we learn when we birth or enlist to be birthed into an earthly being parent becomes lessons we want to learn and share when we come back to this spiritual realm. We also enlist to other planet parents as well. Did you know that?*

V: *Yes, you mentioned two other planets that we haven't even heard of here, but are inhabited. We, on earth, will probably fly there one day when those planets are known and the flights are created.*

Dad: *For years earthlings called those that travel there, aliens. But they're not aliens; they are other life forms. It's earthlings that call them alien merely because they're foreign to their way of life. If earthlings ever do travel between planets like those much more advanced beings, they will know there's a whole different way of living, way beyond what earthlings see from planet earth.*

I, for one, liked it there my last time. I have six wonderful children from that enlistment, and a wife I wished was different, but she served her purpose as the mother of my children. Oh, honey, there are so many children here! I just love children. They're so full of spiritual movement that's exciting and fresh! Similar to a new baby, but here they flit around touching us in various ways.

V: *How so?*

Dad: *It's always beautiful here and so enlightening in a knowledgeable spiritual way, and these little ones telepathically tell us stories of while on earth. Like a sweet cancer patient who left life at age nine. You saw her at her father's store recently. You saw her pictures and two other children but asked the father if he had four children not knowing of a fourth. She was amazed that you said that! She also wants her father to know she wished she could have stayed longer but made sure her father had a new life coming through. She actually told me she didn't want to leave that life before her father and stepmother knew they were to have another child. She said that often happens when a child leaves earth so the grieving parents are kept busy when a child comes back home.*

V: *Amazing! I honestly felt a connection when I saw her picture and said to the father, so do you have four children? He was stymied, paused and said, well yes, I have a son too, but his picture is not there. How did you know? I just felt it from within and said it. He showed me a picture of the little boy, four months old. Hey, there's the four again! Yes, angels were guiding me. Anyway, he showed me a picture of his son and what came out of me was unexpected. I said his eyes tell me he* will speak very young. You need to write down and pay attention to what he says. You know dad, the man Shawn said well, he talked at age two months and said, momma. I told him, I knew and felt he would speak early. Pay attention. The man was not upset but took in what I said. And dad, I had to go back to that store and noted he added the little boy's picture to the group of four children. The girl's name is Faith. What a grand story and you met little Faith.

Dad: Yes, she is delightful, energetic and happy her father and stepmother have a new little one to keep them progressing.

V: Oh, how I love these telepathic discussions. I wish more would learn to meditate and chat with their loved one as I do with you. You do know I talk to you often through prayers. But dad the remarkable fact is that prayer really does work! When I left that cult religion, I never thought I'd pray again as I mentioned earlier. But through all I've studied and learned since reading thousands of books on the subject, I know that prayer is the connection to, not only family but to a vast array of knowledge. I can hardly find enough time to write all I want others to learn about. That's why when I have time to chat with you and type with my eyes shut, I have to make sure my time spent with you is quiet and peaceful. This peacefulness allows me to type quickly making many mistakes I see later, but at least I can correct the typos and still have vast amounts of information from the spiritual side to share with others. You know dad when I stop these sessions with you, I don't recall what I've typed. It's true! I have to reread each session to remember. But the fantastic thing dad, is that when I've told Dwayne and my kids Rachel, Caleb, Blake, and Ashley that I talk to you and they ask me what transpired, all I can recall is that I may have spoken to Debbie or my aunt, but I never remember anything. I wonder why that is.

Dad: *I think it's because there's just so much to remember and when you wake, so to speak, from this meditative discussion with me, life gets in the way immediately and all is forgotten.*

V: *I wonder if that's it. But it must be because you say it's so and I believe you and all others that leave before us have a vast array of knowledge from the spiritual side. I'm so very thankful I've learned to ask, and it's given and that I know how to communicate with you for the next Life after Life book! Amazing! Thank you so very much dad, my loving father!*

You know something is telling me to let this be the final chapter and let others know what I've experienced to date. Yes, that's what I feel and will do. I had no idea I'd stop here.

Dad: *So many will be enlightened to know all they have to do is pray and listen. Listen is the key to learn from beyond. Listen is the key.*

V: *So many on earth, have learned this fantastic aspect of minds and have shared their thoughts in books, which this too, I will share soon. And when I share this, I will continue to chat with you. I'm anxious to learn what the next bit of knowledge is and what I'll glean from you my sweet father, to share what you and other relatives within this spiritual realm of meditation, gift me.*

Love always,

Victoria

V: *Yes, Listen is the key. That might be the title or subheading! From your telepathic voice to my telepathic ears, a new beginning is forming! Till I call upon you again, sooner than before!*

Dad: *Till then. I too love this connection, honey. I don't feel the loss of leaving because you began our sessions a few days after I returned home.*

V: *And I will continue to do so!*

INTRODUCTION SYMBOLS — DECIPHERED

I've taken a great deal of time since the October 28th date, when I found these symbols in the introduction. The way I deciphered the symbols was to hi-light each one in Word, click on the symbol icon under the insert category, and then click on more symbols. After noting the number and digits representing the symbol, I then copied it and pasted into the Internet address bar, thus these interpretations. And I'm not totally sure the interpretation is correct.

◉◉◉◉◉◉◉◉◉◉◉◉◉◉◉◉◉◉◉◉◉◉◉◉◉◉◉◉

◉◉◉◉◉◉◉◉◉◉◉◉◉◉◉◉◉◉◉◉◉◉◉◉◉◉◉◉

◉◉◉◉◉◉◉◉◉◉◉◉◉◉◉◉◉◉◉◉條◉納◉ 緍◉緞◉緣◉縑◉緛◉繍◉縥◉緘◉縺◉纖◉纓◉ 戀◉纟 ▯ ◉◉◉◉◉◉◉◉◉◉◉◉◉◉◉◉◉◉◉◉ 헿 엁 췪 췞 엣 헍 엁 헍 헍 헍 헍 헍 헍 헍 ㄴ

1.) 條   7D5B CJK Unified Ideographs   **Means a fabric SASH in English**
http://jrgraphix.net/r/Unicode/4E00-9FFF

2.) 納   7DC9 **a pair (of shoes)**
https://www.chinese-tools.com/tools/sinograms.html?q=%E7%B7%89

3.) 緍   7DCD Somebody **Old with the " shoes "**

145

Variant of 缗 U+7DE1, a fishing-line; cord; string of coins; a paper or straw string
http://www.zdic.net/z/21/js/7DCD.htm

4.) 緀　7E00　Old with " shoes
http://zidian.kxue.com/zi/xia34.html

5.) 緣　7E01　Hem
http://zidian.kxue.com/zi/yuan51.html

6.) 縑　7E11　a thin silk dress, **fine silk**, the fine weaving of double silk
https://zidian.911cha.com/zi7e11.html

7.) 縓　7E13　Orange or reddish-yellow silk
http://www.zdic.net/z/21/js/7E13.htm

8.) 縤　7E24　"Jade articles" sang cut, oysters also. "The Sea" phonemes. General quality.
http://www.zdic.net/z/21/kx/7E24.htm

9.) 縤　7E24　Health
http://www.zdic.net/z/21/js/7e24.htm

10.) 縥　7E25　The water is in a hurry.
http://www.zdic.net/z/21/js/7E25.htm

11.) 縬　7E2C　Shrink, the color of the silk fabric
https://zidian.911cha.com/zi7e2c.html

12.) 縺　7E3A　1. The wire is entangled 2. An ancient fish net 3. The same with the " connected ."
https://zidian.911cha.com/zi7e3a.html

13.) 纖　7E4A　Fine, delicate, minute, graceful
https://zidian.911cha.com/zi7e4a.html

14.) 緵   7E4C All the internet is translating is: Old with the "緵".
http://www.zdic.net/z/21/js/7E4C.htm
7E4C and this: embroider, ornament
ⁱhttps://zidian.911cha.com/zi7e4c.html

15.) 纞   7E9E constantly
https://zidian.911cha.com/zi7e9e.html

16.) 纟   7E9F Wording - will, English - silk
https://zidian.911cha.com/zi7e9f.html

17.) 헳   D5F3 Hangul Symbol 'helh' - Korea
https://unicode-table.com/en/search/?q=%ED%97%B3

18.) 엍   Hangul Syllable 'Eot'
https://unicode-table.com/en/search/?q=%EC%97%8D

19.) 췕   Hangul Syllable 'Cwelg'
https://unicode-table.com/en/search/?q=%EC%B7%95

20.) 췕   I can't find this one.

21.) 엕   Hangul Syllable 'Enj'
https://unicode-table.com/en/search/?q=%EC%97%95

22.) 헍   Hangul Syllable 'Heonj'
https://www.compart.com/en/unidode/U+D5CD

23.) 엍   Hangul Syllable 'Eot'
https://www.compart.com/en/unicode/U+C5CD

24.) 헍헍헍헍헍헍헍 All are the same symbol Hangul Syllable 'Heonj'
https://www.compart.com/en/unicode/U+D5CD

ᒑ Ṩ Together I can't find anything. Separate ᒑ - when hi-lighted under symbols reads: Unified Canadian Aboriginal Syllabics. Ṩ - also hi-lighted under symbols reads: Latin Extended Additional

These are the symbols that made the most sense to me.

絛7D5B **Sash**

絹7D79 **Thin, tough silk fabric**

緍7DCD **A fishing-line; cord; string of coins; a paper or straw string**

縀7E00 **Old with the "shoes" {I have my father's old shoes! I've had them since August 3rd, 2012! And today would be his 97th birthday - 10-29-18}**

縁7E01 HEM

縑7E11 FINE SILK

縓7E13 **Light red,** English - **Orange or reddish-yellow silk**

縤7E24 HEALTH

縥7E25 THE WATER IS IN A HURRY

縅 7E2C SHRINK

On the next page I located information of the swirl symbol. What grand treats this book has created!

When I copied and pasted this into the internet - ☺☺☺☺☺☺☺☺☺☺☺☺☺☺☺☺☺☺☺☺☺☺☺☺ - it became a rectangle with no info of it. However, the swirl/spiral has several meanings and I found this website of the spiral interesting [ii]https://www.tainoage.com/spirals.html

"According to Carl Jung, the Swiss psychiatrist who founded analytical psychology said that the spiral is an archetypal symbol that **represents cosmic force.**"

◎◎◎◎

2033 ANGEL NUMBER 2033

Number 2033 is a combination of the energies and attributes of the number 2 and 0, and the vibrations of number 3 appearing twice, amplifying its influences and relating to the Master Number 33.

Number 2 relates to duality and balance, diplomacy and adaptability, sensitivity and selflessness. Number 2 also resonates with serving your life purpose and soul mission.

Number 0 amplifies the vibrations of the numbers it appears with and resonates with eternity, infinity, oneness, wholeness, continuing cycles and flow, the beginning point, potential and/or choice, and encourages developing one's spiritual aspects.

Number 3 relates to self-expression and communication, optimism and enthusiasm, friendliness and sociability, growth, expansion and manifesting.

Number 3 relates to the Ascended Masters, who act as mentors, teaching and helping you to find peace, clarity and love within and focus on the Divine spark within yourself and others.

Number 33 is the Master Number 33 (Master Teacher 33), and relates to guidance and assistance, understanding and inner-wisdom, spiritual awakening and the spiritual uplifting of mankind, devotion, compassion, honesty, inspiration and discipline.

Angel Number 2033 brings a message from your angels and the Ascended Masters that they are with you, guiding and assisting you along your Divine life path. Any positive changes or projects you are considering right now will be well worth your while, and you will be assisted in their undertaking. Maintain a positive attitude and high expectations regarding the direction your life is taking and trust that your present course is the right one for you and is aligned with your soul mission and life purpose.

Stay strong in your convictions and listen to your intuition and inner-wisdom.

Angel Number 2033 encourages you to have the courage to live your life with enthusiasm and optimism, safe in the knowledge that you are well blessed, loved and supported in all that you do. Your angels are filling your heart with love, light and faith and you are encouraged to use these loving energies to the betterment of yourself and others, as per your Divine life purpose. Use your natural communication skills, creativity and humour to ease your own stress and that of others and live your life with joy, passion and purpose as this will manifest your true desires. Also be prepared to expand and increase your spiritual awareness at this time, and have faith and trust in yourself and your unique talents and abilities.

The real you is that inner-voice of wisdom that you sometimes hear during moments of clarity; your Higher Self. Listen to it always.

Number 2033 relates to number 8 (2+0+3+3=8) and Angel Number 8.

http://sacredscribesangelnumbers.blogspot.com/2015/04/angel-number-2033.html

10-31-2018 - Something kept telling me these symbols are from my father and other angels!!! I feel I'm correct!

Thank you so much for your insight! I received numerous oriental symbols within a book I'm writing, of my telepathic chats with my father, Wm. Victor Gray, who died in 2012. Three and a half lines of symbols were waiting for me since my last editing early October, to find these symbols on October 28, 2018! I began looking up all symbols and a swirl circle symbol brought me to your site! I knew and know the angels have been helping me almost like a windfall of success since my father left this life journey August 20, 2012. He was and is always a beacon! Victoria Gray - Hay House author 10-31-2018

May I use your information for my book? Life After Life, A grieving daughter's healing chats with her father?

I must have written approval to insert all of the above post on # 2033. Of course, your name and site will be inserted in my book if you approve. Victoria Gray

Life After Life...should be finished by Spring, 2019. Thank you for considering your insert.
All the warmest!

.... And yes, you most certainly do have my permission to use the information you wish (with due credits) in your book.

I wish you the brightest of blessings Victoria, and great success with your upcoming book.   *Joanne*
--
Joanne Walmsley
<u>Sacred Scribes</u>
Intuitive Writer & Lightworker
Information   Inspiration   Enlightenment   Empowerment
Victoria Australia
...
Thank you so very much, Joanne!

I felt I needed more information and texted this to one of my estate sale customers, Ella, who is of Asian descent, on January 17, 2019.

In a text I wrote: Good morn Ella. This is Victoria with estate sales. I wonder if you could possibly decipher these symbols. I've found some online, but not sure if I have their correct meanings. If you don't know them, might you know someone who does?

The below symbols were in a document last October when I went back to work on it the following day. I did not place them there nor do I know where to find them to do so or what they mean. I'm totally puzzled.

Thank you in advance.

Victoria

條7D5B   Sash
絹7D79   Thin, tough silk fabric
緍7DCD   A fishing-line; cord; string of coins; a paper or straw string
緞7E00   Old with the "shoes"
緣7E01   HEM
縑7E11   FINE SILK
縓7E13   **Light red, English - Orange or reddish-yellow silk**
縤7E24   HEALTH
縥7E25   THE WATER IS IN A HURRY
緎7E2C   SHRINK

From Ella: at 12:41 p.m. Some of the characters are Chinese and some are Korean. I don't want to be impolite; may I ask if it comes with something else, because the words stand alone will not make much sense.

...

January 18, 2019; 8:43 p.m. From Ella

緞7Eoo **Old with the "shoes"** It means satin fabric. In old day Chinese use satin to make clothes and shoes. Usually the wealthy people can afford it. "Old with the shoes" does not mean old man shoes. It is general about using satin fabric for shoes.

...

8:47 p.m. To Ella

Awesome! Really awesome!

Thank you so much!

I woke the following morning and realized, perhaps, this is my father's way of telling me how pleased he is with the wedding dress I made for my youngest daughter Ashley, for her September 2, 2018 wedding.

"Good morn Ella.... I woke wondering if you might text what the 1st symbol of each symbol means (like you mentioned yesterday of representing a man), and you also stated something of a wedding, maybe the silk fabrics?"

My father was enthralled with my sewing prowess of over 300 garments for 170 fashion shows I produced from 2005-2014, of which he attended the first. Plus I made my daughter's wedding dress, perhaps this is my father's way of saying bravo to me and that he attended it posthumously. I'd like to think so....

That same evening Ella texted this: "The word you sent to me, it is the kind of cloth you can use for wedding dresses. Usually the shoes will be the match. I don't know whether this helps."

After my texts back and forth with Ella, I truly believe my father sent the symbols.

I know I could call upon my father to tell me if in fact he sent these symbols, however after all this research and knowledge, I *feel* I might do it unfairly. Thus, here's my take on each symbol.

條7D5B **Sash** (Ashley bought a pre-beaded design, which I hand sewed onto a sash for her to wear around the wedding waist once she removed the train.)

絹7D79 **Thin, tough silk fabric** (The lining looked like silk and was a tougher fabric for strength under the sheer see through overlay netting.)

緡7DCD **A fishing-line; cord; string of coins; a paper or straw string** (The sash was a fine cord with strings of beads and sequins costing coins.)

緞7E00 **Old with the "shoe's".** {I have my father's old shoes! I've had them since August 3rd, 2012, and today would be his 97th birthday - 10-29-18} (I learned this represented wedding shoes made of fine silk and not my father's physical shoes.)

緣7E01 **HEM** (I certainly applied a hem with lace around the base of the wedding dress, the sheer overlay and the eight-foot train.)

縑7E11 **FINE SILK** (The overlay netting was like sewing on fine silk and just as tedious.)

縓7E13 **Light red, English - Orange or reddish-yellow silk** (The wedding clearly had none of these colors or hues, however the sunset certainly did!)

縼7E24 HEALTH (Maybe this one represents my son's ill health at the wedding, so noted in the symbol via dad.)

縥7E25 THE WATER IS IN A HURRY (This one made me chuckle. The wedding took place on a yacht off the Chicago peer and perhaps the water was in a hurry that day. The chuckle came from the wedding and reception. Each event had a time stamp on it. We hurriedly ate to allow time for the first dance on the upper deck to hear my son Caleb sing a special song he wrote, titled My Dreamer (hear him on my website: iv www.victoriagray.net).
The photos had a time allotment as did chatting. All took place within a four-hour trip. Yes, we hurried and scurried about that day, to be sure!)

縬7E2C SHRINK (Possibly, this represents the fact that once I thought I'd finished the wedding dress, and did the final fitting, it seemed Ashley's waist shrunk from a size four to a two. I had to add tucks at the back of the waist.)

I'm sure dad saw it all; similarly to the hospital visits I had with him and represented his thoughts posthumously, via symbols.

List of those that came forward

V – Victoria Gray

D – Dad – William Victor Gray

Deb – Debbie Gray – my sister that passed in 1997

F – Fidella – Grandmother Gray

T – Theodore – Grandfather Gray

Tessie – my aunt and dad's favorite sister

ABOUT THE AUTHOR

Victoria Gray discovered the passion of writing as her father taught her to read and write by the tender age of four-and-a-half. Since that time, she tests all pens for a smooth run over the paper, and equally, the paper must compete with the smoothness of the pen.

Her ability to intuit and receive from the ethers began when Victoria, during her fourteenth year almost succumbed to a violent electric shock that brought her to her knees. From that time hence, during a mixture of times and while working at diverse estate sale setups, she often sees, feels, and or hears someone from the other side, immediately jotting notes of such.

Consequently when her dear father died August of 2012, face to face chatting halted; thus a meditative transference of communication was in order.

After leaving a strict religious background, her intuitive voice blossomed. Inhibitions of life after life subsided. Henry Ford came to her via a dream, informing her of his first home, his first car plant and various other aspects of his life. Because of this dream's factual basis, Victoria studied dreams at the School of Metaphysics, thus enlightened of something more; a new age of thought began. She also studied at the local college; screenwriting, play-writing and cinematography, in her spare time.

She became the Vice-President of the local writer's guild for a 1-year term, and is consistently working on future books. Forthcoming are: My Past Life with Henry Ford, and The Secret Vision – The Richness of Thought.

She lives in St. Louis, and is the mother of four with one grandson and another little one, a girl, on the way.

Visit her at: www.victoriagray.net

Gray's Titles of Related Interest

ESTATE SALES MADE EASY - A
Practical Guide to Success From Start to Finish, Victoria Gray

Hay House

THE SECRET VISION

The Richness of Thought, Victoria Gray

Gray publishing (Fall 2019)

MY PAST LIFE WITH HENRY FORD

Victoria Gray – Gray publishing (December 2019)

www.victoriagray.net

THE ANKLE EXPRESS – Life and Times of Wm. Victor Gray

Gray publishing

theankleexpress.com

VICTORIA GRAY UNFOLDED

The Speaking Linens

Gray publishing

www.amazon.com

Endnotes

i http://bible.cfmin.com/PAYATTENTION.pdf

ii https://www.sciencedirect.com/science/article/abs/pii/S0043135499003759

iii https://www.tainoage.com/spirals.html

iv www.victoriagray.net

theankleexpress.com

www.amazon.com

Made in the USA
Monee, IL
06 November 2023